# Master The Game

*Become the King of Car Sales*

TAREQ Z. SAQQA

ISBN: 1500366080
ISBN 13: 9781500366087
Library of Congress Control Number: 2014912290
Createspace Independent Publishing Platform
North Charleston, South Carolina

# Welcome

Welcome to the car game! If you're reading this book, you're probably new to the car business, or maybe you've been in the car business for a while but you are interested in reading some new material that explores different ways to step up your game. Well, to all you salespeople out there, whether you're new or you're a veteran, I'm happy to have your attention! Welcome to the club, boys and girls. This is the world where deals are made and commissions get paid every time a hand gets shaken—a place where we turn curious shoppers into delighted buyers. We work in an environment that allows us the unique opportunity to interact with all types of people each and every day. It's here that we face new challenges while working on the fly in an adrenaline-filled workplace where we are constantly learning something new. I don't know if you've realize it yet, but *you* have been lucky enough to find your way into one of the most unique, exciting, fast-paced, and *most lucrative* professions in the world!

In this day and age, vehicles have become a necessity rather than a luxury. **Everyone is driving a car.** With all the updated technology and evolving financing options, it is easier today for people to own cars. Therefore, the car market is consistently growing, and it's now stronger than it's ever been. The potential earnings for salespeople have never been better. So get your head in the game, because it's grinding time. Jump on this opportunity to take your career to places you've previously never thought possible.

You don't need a diploma or any type of degree to be a salesperson. These days most dealerships offer free on-the-job training. Look for a dealership with a great management team that will give you the opportunity to go from making average wages to becoming a superstar who earns an annual income comparable to doctors, engineers, and lawyers. That's right—I'm talking six figures! The average annual Canadian income is $46K to $48K. I currently have salespeople on my floor making double that and then some. But the magic dust that makes all this possible can't just be given to you. *You* must look deep inside your soul and ask yourself, "Do I have the will to win, the drive to be number one, and the ability to do all the things that others won't?"

I believe in you, but you must also believe in yourself. You have already taken the first step alone. Now let's walk the rest of the journey together. That's selling!

# Introduction

Before we begin, I'd like to tell you how I came to the decision to embark on a new journey of writing and publishing my first book.

I'm an avid book reader. I love all types of books and all different types of genres, from business and marketing all the way to fiction and fantasy. I have an amazing wife and a young baby boy who puts a smile on my face every time I see him. I like sports but not enough to talk about them. I am a family man driven by success, but above all else, my true passion is cars. I'm a car guy. I love driving all different makes and models, and I also love talking about cars as much as I love selling them. Cars are my true passion, as well as my career path. But I have to say, I am treading through uncharted territory right now in publishing a book. However, I just feel like I have to get my knowledge of dealing cars out there. I mean, sure, I have a passion for English, but to write a book—well, that's taking it to a whole new level. So in order to make a statement, I've taken on this new challenge to do something different and to take a huge leap out of my comfort zone in attempting something I've never done before.

When the idea of writing this book first shot through my brain like a bolt of lightning, my first thought to myself was, *Wow! What a great sense of accomplishment I will feel if I can pull this off.* As I pictured myself holding my newly published book, I thought of the long road to the finish line. I started to visualize how I would get it done. Of course, after all of these warm and fuzzy feelings, a few opposing thoughts came to mind.

I thought to myself, *Do I really want to invest so many hours writing a book? Do I really want to take on this project with my busy schedule? What business do I have writing a book in the first place? Is there room for me up there with all the great authors?* After questioning myself, I decided to block out all negative energy and negative thoughts, and instead opted to follow the path that would pay out the greater reward. After rationalizing my idea and actually giving myself a realistic time frame for completion, I started to feel like writing a book was going to be a fun challenge, and so I started to put my plan in motion.

The main purpose of this book is to show that you don't need to be wealthy to get a book published, nor do you need an English literature degree to write one. All you need is a motive, a plan, and a goal. With those three elements, anyone can do anything he or she wants. It may be writing a book, running a marathon, getting to your ideal weight, or becoming more successful than you ever thought possible. It doesn't matter what the goal is. All that matters is the focus and energy you put into realizing that goal. For me personally, writing this book is a true testament to the old phrase "Make sure you see it through."

On a regular Sunday afternoon that just so happened to be the Sunday a couple of days before the start of 2014, I was sitting in my bonus room with a fresh cup of coffee, and I was about to start reading a book that had been referred to me by one of my mentors called *It's Not How Good You Are, It's How Good You Want to Be*, written by Paul Arden. As I sat there, I kept reading the cover page over and over. Then I thought to myself how I keep reading book after book, written by great authors, about business and success, always looking to find things that I can relate to—information and ideas that speak to me and tie into my life and what I'm about. Book after book, I read on, filtering through each one, extracting all the information that I find useful to me, and then using it to better myself and increase my knowledge of the world and all aspects of life, whether the information relates to business, attitude, self-motivation tools, health and image, or an entrepreneur's road to success. I have gotten the chance to see the world through the eyes of very renowned men and women, who have created their own successes in life and have chosen to share, through literature, how they got to where they are.

After it all, I said to myself, *What if I were to write a book and keep the focus on car sales, not on sales in general?* Although a book on general sales practices would attract a wider market and more readers, I decided that was not my goal.

My purpose is to reach out to all of you in the car dealing industry who are looking for ways to become stronger, more ferocious salespeople. Also to those of you who are just getting your foot in the door, this book will allow you to get a real sense of the industry and find out exactly what it takes to sell cars. I want to relate to all of you through my own experiences. I want to share with the world (or whoever's listening) the guidelines I personally follow that make me so successful, the frame of mind I maintain in sales, and also the process I use that I believe in enough to want to publish. I'm going to give you some tips and organizational tools along the way that will help you become the top-performing salesperson in your dealership and will help you carve out the road to your success.

This book will give you the how-to on car sales. In the first chapter, my main focus is on attitude. Having the right attitude and staying in the right frame of mind are two of the most important factors that come into play if you want to make it big in this car dealing game. In the second chapter, I break down my selling process—my seven steps of selling—that I use as my guideline. In Chapter 3, I get into the almighty follow-up. Here I show you guys the most effective ways to follow up to ensure that you make an impact on your guest. My fourth chapter focuses on the power of the telephone. In the car business, the telephone is your strongest tool, and once you realize that and learn how to master using it, you will increase your business astronomically. In Chapter 5, I discuss the Internet and how big of a role it plays in the car industry. In my sixth and final chapter, I focus on motive. If you want to become a powerhouse on the sales floor, this chapter suggests things you should be doing more often as well as the things you should never be doing.

So what's your motive? What goals have you set for yourself? What makes you wake up every morning with your game face on? How far up the ladder do you want to climb? I'll keep you driven, day in and day out, so that you wake up every morning ready to take on the world and achieve a level of success you believe you can achieve.

Special thanks to John Kalogeras for giving me a seat at the leadership table and teaching me everything I know.

# Contents

# Chapter 1:
# Attitude

*"Don't stop till your heart stops." – John Kalogeras*

Good morning!

1. Brush teeth…check

2. Shower…check

3. Put on fresh outfit…check

4. Eat breakfast…check

5. Put shoes on…check

6. Grab cell phone…check

7. Grab car keys…check

8. **Check attitude…check!**

I'm going to kick off the first chapter and get to the thing that's most important for you to learn if you are ever going to become successful. That's right, ladies and gentlemen. It's all about your **attitude**! I preach this day in and day out. People don't want to deal with individuals who are negative. If you have a bad attitude and you are always thinking and saying negative things, slap yourself in the face right now! You deserved that. Now that we got that out of the way, let's get back to business.

Every action you take stems from your attitude. That's why attitude is the first step in my "Seven Steps of Selling" that I will discuss in more depth in Chapter 2. Because having the right attitude is vital to your success, I've chosen to give it a chapter all its own. The better and stronger your attitude, the better and stronger your actions will be. When you have the right attitude and you are always in a good mood, you will attract others to you in a positive way. You will notice that more people will want to deal with you and not the next guy just based off the energy you can create by being positive.

When you have a positive attitude you see things differently. You have a different mindset when dealing with any situation. When your attitude is positive, you are always looking for ways to better yourself and those around you. If you always have a good attitude, things will just seem to go your way. It's not because you are lucky; it's because you've trained your mind to attract the things you want. Someone with a positive attitude who doesn't believe in negative thinking can turn a negative situation into a positive one by simply finding the positive in the negative and bringing it to the surface.

Successful sales people have strong characteristics. They are upbeat, humorous, dedicated, motivated, and well spoken, and they are able to engage in conversation with anyone at anytime. Successful salespeople are able to manage themselves and their time effectively. You'll know that includes you when you start saying things to yourself like "I wish I had two more hours" or "Oh, man, it's already five o'clock." These are common phrases that come from people who are highly productive and focused on producing, and those are good traits to have. On the other hand, if you catch yourself staring at your watch during a shift, that's a huge red flag. It's not like you are a grass-seed analyst who gets paid to watch grass grow—boring. If you feel like you don't have anything to do and find yourself just sitting around, then *find* something to do. Ask your manager for some leads, make some follow-up calls, and study your inventory so you are ready for the next opportunity that walks through the door. There's no such thing as nothing to do. Make something happen! Don't be that person. If you think that you can sit around and wait for deals to fall into your lap, it's not going to happen. You will never be more than an average salesperson. Remember, you are not getting paid hourly. This is a commission-based job!

In this business, you deal with different personalities every day, and you need to be able to adapt to and connect with every one you meet. The better you get at doing that, the easier it will be for you to succeed. Your mindset going into any conversation or situation needs to be positive. You always need to be friendly and approach every one with a smile. But don't be mistaken; that's just the first step. It may sound easy enough, but the second thing you need to be able to do is stay in control in any situation. You are the one driving the sales bus to the finish line. Your friendliness is what's going to help you get there. The more product knowledge you possess, as well as the ability to walk your guest through the sales process step by step, the smoother the ride becomes for the both of you.

There's an unsung rule in the car business. *Leave your problems at the door!* You can't come to work upset and expect to be productive. If you are in a bad mood or upset for whatever personal reason, you need to learn how to check those issues at the door, because once you step foot into the dealership, it's show time. If you can't learn to control those negative thoughts and feelings, you will set yourself up to have a bad day. You will become less friendly to all of your coworkers. Also, it will be less likely that you'll be able to befriend the next opportunity that walks through the door. At that point not only are you hurting yourself, your negativity is now affecting the whole dealership. Again, don't be that person. If you have personal problems, deal with them away from work; use the dealership as your escape point if you have to. Your fellow employees don't want to hear about your problems; everyone in the dealership is there to perform and produce. There's no time to play shrink. If it's that big of an issue and you just can't shake it, go talk to your manager let him or her know what's going on and take some time off to deal with it.

# CHAPTER 1: ATTITUDE

Control your attitude. It's not easy to stay positive day in and day out, but it's something you need to master. Surround yourself with positive people. Don't allow negative individuals to influence you. If you find someone at your workplace whom you find to be a pessimist, stay away from that person. Don't get caught in a circle jerk or find your way into a negative conversation, where one guy is complaining about something that he doesn't feel to be fair, and the next guy is agreeing with everything he's saying, and all the while you're acknowledging their comments. Stop it! Don't get sucked in. If you do, you are just as negative as they are. As a top performer, you should be too busy selling cars that you don't have time to get involved with that stuff anyway.

Misery loves company. Someone with a negative attitude, who's always moaning and groaning and always finding something to complain about, can cause a rippling effect throughout the dealership. Customers can easily pick up on negative attitudes, and once they sense that vibe, they will be less likely to make a purchase.

The world has created a stereotype about salespeople, and it's not a good one. Word is we are a pushy, sleazy, untrustworthy group of people. Just remember, it's only a stereotype. So when the wall is up, remember it's only because most people simply don't know any better. It's your job, then, to be the opposite. Go into every sale with a great attitude and have your customer's best interests in mind. Break down the wall by finding out exactly what it is your guests are trying to accomplish. They could be looking to upgrade their vehicle or maybe just reduce their payment. It could be any reason, and it doesn't matter. Just find out their reason for being in your dealership, and help them accomplish what they came to get done. If you genuinely care about your guests' experience, your volume will go through the roof!

Always keep in mind that this is an industry of customer service. Not only that, we typically have the toughest clientele to please. If you have a guest who you are dealing with and he or she doesn't like you, what are the odds of that guest trusting you enough to make a purchase from you? Slim to none. It's very easy for that guest to pick up and leave your store and simply head to the dealership across the street instead. There is competition everywhere. You need to be able to genuinely make everyone feel comfortable in order to charm your way into a car deal. If you are dealing with a tough costumer who has his or her defense wall set up from the moment he or she steps into your dealership, it's your attitude that will determine where this potential sale will go. Don't let that tough customer break you! Stay positive and energetic, keep in control, and find common ground, and you'll slowly start to break down the wall and win the customer over. Next thing you know, the customer's laughing, and you are laughing, and boom, he or she is signing a bill of sale. Not only did that customer buy from you, he or she will more than likely thank you for being a breath of fresh air.

## I'm Going to Close Everyone

You are either with a customer, or waiting for one. When you are on top of your game, everything is going right, and everyone you run into is a potential buyer!

You are going to run into different types of buyers. Some are impulse buyers, while others are not so impulsive. An impulsive buyer is quick to make a decision. Impulse buyers make their purchases based off of emotion. All you need to do is find them a vehicle that hits their hot buttons and make it totally affordable, and then you got yourself a deal. They don't need much time to think about the purchase. They don't need to ask their friends or family members if they think the car purchase is a good deal. They just need a vehicle and want to feel good about you and their purchase. Impulse buyers are kind of an easy sell.

On the other hand, we have nonimpulsive buyers—still a great type of buyer. When nonimpulsive buyers seek to purchase a vehicle, they usually start by doing their research on the Internet. From there, they decide what makes and models they think they would be interested in. They then find a couple of dealerships that have their desired vehicle in stock. Most customers usually start with the car with the lowest price, or sometimes their favorite color preference. They will come out to test drive the vehicle with you. Because they are still in the early stages of their shopping, nonimpulsive buyers will not commit to buying your vehicle even though they really liked it. You are more than likely going to hear things like "I still have two more to look at" or "I really like the car, but I still need to do my research on it."

As a salesperson, those are two infamous lines we never like to hear, right? Well, this is where a little experience can really help you out. It's OK! You can sit there and try to hammer them to a bill of sale. You can try to close them with closing lines like "Oh, you still need to look at two more? Fantastic! Just real quick before you go, tell me, was my vehicle missing anything for you?" By asking that question, you open the door to finding out what the guest's objection is to making a purchase. Once you find out the objection, this gives you another opportunity to overcome it. But I'll get in to that later on in the book. The point I'm getting at is that it's OK to let your guest leave. As you become a stronger salesperson, it will be easier for you to understand and be aware that sometimes even the greatest closers can't close a guest who just sincerely wants to look at another vehicle at a different dealership, or who wants to consult with a family member before committing to making a purchase. It's OK! Wouldn't it be better to give your guest all the information they requested, help them out as much as you can, and make sure that when they leave your dealership they leave with a good impression? This will increase your odds of them coming back to buy. And if they do come back, then they will be back to close the deal! At that point it's just a matter of following up with them and making sure they come through.

> *Tip: Identifying what type of guest you are dealing with as soon as possible will help you close everyone. The key is that you can't expect to close everyone on your first encounter.*

You are going to run into various obstacles with various guests. For the most part, these obstacles are all the same. Sometimes it's just a matter of a guest wanting a specific vehicle that you don't currently have in stock. You can try to switch the guest to another vehicle, but if he or she is dead set on a certain make and model, sometimes that guest is not switchable. Again, get all of the guest's information, answer all of his or her questions, and let the guest leave with a good impression of you and your dealership. Then your hunt can begin in trying to locate the guest's desired vehicle before he or she finds it somewhere else. If you leave your guest with a really good impression, he or she will even wait for you to find the vehicle—but only for so long!

Frequently, when you are working a car deal, you are working a deal that has a trade involved. That trade can turn out to be the deciding factor in whether or not you close the deal. A lot of guests come in thinking that their vehicle is worth more than it actually is. There is a proper appraisal process that you should go through, as well as a devaluing process that will help your guests understand why their vehicle is worth what the dealership is prepared to pay. I'll get into trade appraisals a little later on.

There are going to be times where you will run into people who have a lot of negative equity. That's not the tough part. Negative equity can be buried, but in most cases it has to be on a newer vehicle, causing the customer's monthly payment to likely increase. These are good things to know so that you can explain them to your guest prior to him or her selecting a vehicle. Some guests will be open to a higher payment, while others will be a little harder to stretch.

# CHAPTER 1: ATTITUDE

Some guests are going to be limited to a certain amount of money the bank will lend them. These are most likely subprime customers, or prime customers who only make x amount of money per month, so the bank will decide what they can afford monthly. This is called debt ratio. The bank calculates monthly income along with rent or mortgage payment and other payments and tells someone what he or she should be paying for a monthly car payment. The purpose of this is to keep someone in a comfortable payment so that there is a lower risk of that person defaulting on payments. That being the case, it's good to be aware of debt ratio so that when you are dealing with customers, you can make them aware of this and remind them that banks are the ones lending them money, not you.

Subprime customers are a little bit easier to deal with. They know that they have had credit issues in the past and are aware that they are probably going to be paying a little bit of a higher interest rate. A lot of times they are just looking for a vehicle that fits their lifestyle and meets the bank's requirements, and they are often looking for an opportunity to reestablish their credit. The great thing about subprime lenders is that there are really good programs for second-time financing. So for every subprime customer you sell to, you can look forward to a future deal down the road!

Prime customers, on the other hand, have the advantage of being able to buy a vehicle anywhere they want, and they know it. They are aware of the fact that they have good credit, so when prime guests go shopping for a vehicle, they want to get a great deal. This is where your positive attitude and charisma come into play. Make sure that these guests have a great experience with you. You need to earn their trust throughout the sales process so that when you ask for the sale they will trust you enough to say yes!

Customers like to deal with salespeople who know their stuff. They want to be guided throughout their purchase. For us, it's everyday things. A car buyer only purchases a vehicle every couple of years, if not longer. They are not familiar with the process, and they often don't know what to

9

expect. They aren't aware of how easy it is to get insurance and register a vehicle. These days most dealerships set these things up in-house. These are the types of things that you should be explaining to your guests in order to take some of the weight of their purchase of their backs.

Confidence comes with knowledge. The more you know about your inventory, financing options, and the types of customers you will encounter, the stronger salesperson you will become. It's one thing to talk to the talk, but you must walk the walk as well. That's what separates the good from the great. You need to create a vibe around yourself that lets everyone know that you are the best. You want a customer to walk into your dealership and want to deal with *you*. Take every opportunity you get and make the best of it. Find a way to make a deal happen. Have a great attitude, stay positive, and let your energy and charisma get you your next car deal.

## Believe That You Are the Best

- Believe in yourself

- Believe in your management team

- Believe in your product

- Believe in your company

- Believe in your customer service

*"Until you believe you are the best, you will never be the best."*

*"To be a great champion, you must believe that you are the best. If you're not, pretend you are." – Muhammad Ali*

# CHAPTER 1: ATTITUDE

### *Believe in Yourself*

Only the strong survive. Be prepared to go through ups and downs, good times and bad times. At the end of the day the only thing that matters is that you believe in yourself and your abilities. Can you really be the best if you don't believe that you are?

A huge part of your attitude relies on your belief system. Once you believe that you're the best, you're going to start acting like the best. That's what matters. When you're in that state of mind, not only are your co-workers going to recognize it, but so are your guests. Your success depends on how confident you are. Confidence comes with knowledge. The more you know, the more confident you will be. The more time you spend in the industry, the more situations you're going to have to deal with. That's one of the best things about the business. You're always dealing with different situations with any given guest. So once you deal with a situation for the first time, when you find yourself in the same situation next time around, you will know how to deal with it. This type of confidence obviously can't be built overnight. Time and experience are what will get you there.

Don't get me wrong. For all you salespeople who are new to the industry, your lack of experience doesn't mean you can't be confident. Don't buckle when a guest asks you a question you don't have the answer to or when you find yourself in a situation you don't know how to handle. It's OK! That's what you have a manager for. The worst thing you can do is lie or make something up that you think sounds good. It may work once or twice. Eventually, though, you will get called out by a guest who came prepared, and once you do, you will lose all credibility as well as you're chances of closing a car deal. The right thing to do is to be honest. It's not a bad thing to look your guest in the face and tell him or her, "Hey, that's a great question, but I'm not sure what the right answer is, so why don't I grab my manager. I'm sure he can help us figure it out!" This way you gain the support of your manager through his involvement, and at the same time you give your guest a solid answer. You need to understand that it's OK not to have all the answers; we are human, after all. If you have a good enough relationship with your guest, that person will totally understand when you say that you're unsure. Not only that, your guest will respect you and trust you more when you go out of your way to get them a straight, honest answer instead of giving them a not-so-educated guess. The harder you work for your guests, the more they will want to make their purchase with you.

Believe in your ability to sell. Don't let a tough customer throw you off. You are going to come across some guests who are obnoxious, rude, and arrogant, and some who simply just don't like you. There are many different personalities out there. You're not going to click with everyone. Don't lose your cool, though. And don't stoop to their level either. Very politely, ask them if they would prefer to deal with a different sales associate, or get your manager involved right away. Let your manager decide whether or not you have a serious buyer on your hands or someone who has just decided to use you as a punching bag.

For the most part, guests just want to be taken care of. They will have their needs and wants. You need to be able to sit down with people and find out exactly why they are searching for a new vehicle and what's most important to them. You then have to be able to separate their needs from their wants. You also need to be able to find out what features are a must-have for them and what features they can go without.

*Example 1*: A guest tells you he is looking for a work truck and it must be a 4x4. That 4x4 option is going to be the deal breaker for him. If that's the deal breaker, I would then look to find out if he's open to all makes and models as long as they come equipped with the 4x4 option. This allows you to expand your search to all makes and models as opposed to just one.

*Example 2*: A guest tells you that she needs a fast and reliable vehicle, but it has to be fuel efficient. You then ask the guest how important fuel efficiency is to her, and she tells you that it's the most important thing. Well, this one should be a no-brainer. The compromise will be that the guest will need to look at vehicles with smaller engines, like a 1.8L–2.0L four-cylinder to maximize fuel-saving potential. These vehicles aren't typically built for speed.

*Example 3*: A guest tells you that he is looking to trade off his current vehicle so that he can lower his current monthly payment. Once you identify that lowering his payment is his primary objective, you can bet that your guest will be willing to compromise on the types of vehicles you can show him that will help him achieve this objective.

There is always a motive. The more often you can find it, the easier it will be for you to understand what it is that will make your guests agree to purchase from you.

Always remember, as long as you have your guests' best interest in mind, and you genuinely love to help people find their perfect vehicle, you will be a great salesperson. Your ability to sell cars is more than just being able to deal with tough guests. That's just one aspect of your job. The main thing you need to realize is that there is a huge demand for vehicles, new or used. People buy cars every day for multiple reasons. That's great news for you! As long as you have a great attitude and an effective sales process, you are going to sell cars—it's inevitable. Understanding that fact and not letting your attitude deteriorate when things don't go your way is probably the biggest thing most salespeople struggle with. So if you want to be the best, tell yourself that you are the best. You have the ability to sell cars. Just stick to your process and keep on selling.

To be great takes time and practice. As long as you believe in yourself and truly believe that this is what you want to do as a career, then keep on learning, and keep showing up to work ready to get the job done. Always look for new ways to better yourself and move forward in your career. If you have that mentality, you will one day get to sit on the throne and say, "I'm the best!"

## *Believe in Your Management Team*

To become a great salesperson, you must have the proper guidance. A great management team will help you reach your full potential. Look for a management team that's hands on and always willing to help you. A great management team should guide you toward reaching your goals as well as helping you reach goals that you would never think to be attainable.

Your manager should be your strongest tool. The more involved your manager is with you and your deals, the more deals you will close. Two heads are better than one. You may not necessarily need to get your manager involved with every deal, but his or her involvement will always help. At the very least your manager should say hello to every guest that you have in the store so that your guests feel like they are being taken care of. As a customer in any establishment, it always feels good when the manager comes by to say hello. It creates a sense of significance. You want every guest to feel like he or she is getting exclusive treatment. If you can get your guest emotionally high on feeling important, you will put them in a buying mood!

Use your manager to help you get great. You should be able to ask your manager what he or she thinks of your performance. If there are some areas in the sales process where you are a little weak, it's good for you to know these areas and get some feedback on how to improve so that you know what you need to focus on come training time. There's nothing wrong with constructive criticism; even the strongest salespeople get criticized. It's all about how you take it. Never let your ego get in the way of learning or trying something new. A know-it-all attitude is the worst attitude you can have. Believe me when I tell you, if you think you know it all, you're wrong. In this industry, you better adapt or die, because process, inventory, and demand are always changing.

### *Believe in Your Product*

How well do you know what you're selling? Do you think you have a great product? What makes your product superior compared to your competitors' product?

There's nothing worse than dealing with salespeople who don't have the slightest clue about what their selling. Think back to the last time you were in a furniture store or an electronics store looking to make a purchase, and you got stuck with a salesperson who couldn't answer any of your questions. Or even worse, the salesperson was making up answers to cover up for his or her lack of product knowledge. You probably ended up leaving with a less-than-average experience, and at the very best, you may have come away satisfied.

Thinking about lack of product knowledge from that perspective, think about how your guests' experience would be if they had to deal with you and you didn't have a clue about any of the vehicles on your lot. If you are still new to the business, lack of product knowledge is understandable. You certainly can't expect to learn your product inside and out overnight. You can play the "new guy" card for a little while, but eventually that card will expire.

If you're selling new or used cars, you better do your homework. You will never be the best if you don't put your time in and study your vehicles. The more you know about your inventory, the easier it will be for you to sell it. Not only that, customers like when you have all the answers to all of their questions. It lets them know that you're prepared and professional and that you mean business. You have to be full of confidence and knowledge so that every customer you earn leaves feeling the same way about his or her purchase.

Selling new cars is a little bit different than selling used cars. When you're in new car sales, you need to memorize all the options and trim levels on all the manufactured products. It's important to understand that options cost money. So the higher the trim level, the more cash your guest is going to have to cough up. This is good to know if you have a guest who's payment conscious, and in those cases, it's probably best to start with a base model.

Every year manufacturers release new lines of vehicles, all packed with new options, so your studying will never end. Usually manufacturers have training courses on their new products. These training sessions are a great way to get the sales team excited and ready to push that metal.

You also need to be aware of new car rebates and incentives. All different makes and models offer different rebates and incentives at any given time. Make sure you stay aware of these breaks, and keep yourself updated on the latest programs. Customers have access to all that kind of information on the Internet, so don't be surprised when they bring it up during the sale.

Selling used cars is a whole different world. You don't have to memorize any brochures, and you don't have to worry about rebates and all that fun stuff. You get the opportunity to sell all different types of vehicle makes and models. You get to sell domestic vehicles, import vehicles, and luxury vehicles. There is a huge variety. The great part about used car sales is that you're not expected to know every single make and model, including trim levels, inside and out. It's easier to get away with not knowing the answer to a simple question like "What's the engine size in this vehicle?" If you're unsure about the answer, you could say, "I'm not sure, but I see all different makes and models on the daily. Let's pop the hood and find out!"

---

*Tip: If you're selling a car that you're not so familiar with, if you have some time before your appointment, go on the Internet and research the car a little. Give yourself a little bit of an edge on your guest prior to presenting the car. You can't go wrong.*

---

In the used car market, there will always be vehicles that are new to you. The more experience and time you get under your belt, the more vehicles you will get a chance to lay your eyes on and become familiar with. If you want to be the best at what you do, don't wait for your manager to train you. If you ever have any downtime during your work day, going on the Internet and researching cool information about cars will take you a lot farther than burning your spare time on social media networks. That's a promise!

When selling new or used cars, your attitude toward your product needs to be the same. You need to believe that you have the greatest, most dominant product on the market. It's one thing to say it, but it's another thing to actually believe it. When you believe in your product and you're passionate about it, you will sell it easier because your passion will be oozing out of your skin during every pitch, every presentation, every test drive, and most importantly, every close. This is what it takes to be great—a belief system and a passion that you can express to each and every customer you talk to, so much so that you never allow them to tell you no. Welcome to the world of selling!

## Believe in Your Company

The greater the corporation you work with, the greater the benefits are for you. In the car industry, there are a wide variety of companies, from corner lots all the way to massive nationwide corporations. You need to ask yourself, *Which one of these groups do I want to be a part of?* Smaller dealerships or even corner lots are great places to work and earn a living. You have just as fair a shot at making a living in these businesses as you would with a huge company, but how far in your career can you really go? Do smaller outlets offer any room for growth?

A good company is always expanding. The more profitable they become, the more they will expand, leaving you with real opportunity for advancement. This is a great attribute to look for if you're thinking of making a change in employment. A good company also offers benefits to you and your family, such as health care, fair vacation times, and great investment programs. At a good company, you will be able to build a solid reputation and have the support of your company behind you.

As a salesperson, you want to find a big company with a great reputation. The larger the company and the better their reputation, the greater the clientele base they will have. That's a good thing for you. No need to tell you why. Not only will you have a larger clientele base to sell from, you will also have an unlimited resource of vehicles to select from. There's nothing worse than working at a dealership that can't keep up with your demand then having to go tell your guest that you will call him or her when you find the vehicle he or she is looking for. This is bound to happen if the guest is looking for a rare or specific vehicle, and you can't get your hands on one at the time, but if you find yourself in that situation more often than not, there's a problem. Get yourself out of that situation quickly. One of the biggest reasons the average closing ratio on walk-in traffic is so low is because we aren't able to land our guests on the right vehicle. The more vehicles you have to choose from, the easier selling becomes.

# CHAPTER 1: ATTITUDE

To be the biggest and the strongest you need to work with the biggest and the strongest. Don't sell yourself short. If you have any doubt about the company you work for, leave it. You are a representative of your company. You need to believe in the company you work for so that you can represent a place that means something to you and work in an environment that maximizes your full potential.

## *Believe in Your Customer Service*

In the world of sales, customer service is the only thing that matters. This means that you better be taking care of your guests, or someone else will. Not only are we in the sales industry, but we are in the car sales industry. And in the car business, we have the toughest clientele to please. After all, the horror stories, bad experiences, and so-called lemons that are out there. Customers are very concerned before entering car dealerships. It's up to you to be able to turn them into trusting buyers, and that all depends on how great your customer service is.

What makes you better than your competitor? What are you willing to do that your competitor isn't? When you think about customer service, what comes to mind? It's the service provided by you to your customer. Customers in the car market just want to get a good deal, and at the same time they want to feel happy and comfortable with their purchase. Whether they are looking to buy a new vehicle or a preowned vehicle, they want to feel that they've been taken care of. They want to be able to buy a car from you and know that if anything happens you will be there to help them out. That doesn't mean you have to pay for their tow bills or car repairs. It just means that you need to be available to answer any of their questions. We are car people. We deal with different situations every day. But most of our customers aren't so car savvy. They may not know the answers to questions that we are frequently asked. Taking care of customers is what good customer service is all about.

A lot of salespeople out there don't care about their guests. They just see dollar signs, and the relationship with a customer ends the minute they screw that license plate on and say good-bye. That's too bad for those guys! They are missing out on big opportunities for repeat and referral business.

You need to capitalize on every opportunity you can to not just sell a car but to build a relationship with your guests so that they spread the word about you to all of their family and friends. That's what going to get you to higher volumes than you ever imagined. You do that through great customer service.

Think outside the box. Try to make every deal a special one. One thing that's very important is that you be true to your word. If you make a promise to one of your guests, you better follow through. The easiest way to lose credibility is through an unfulfilled promise. Go the extra mile for your guests. A great way to earn a relationship is by doing more than what was asked from you. A little extra goes a long way.

For example, let's say you sell a vehicle to a family and you overhear one of the children on a test drive saying how he can't wait to watch his favorite cartoon on the DVD player that comes equipped in the vehicle. Upon delivery, you give the family the keys, shake their hands, and soon they are on their way. On the ride home, they turn the DVD player on, and they notice that you bought them their child's favorite DVD and put it the DVD player for them. Not only will they appreciate your kindness, but they will definitely remember you the next time they are in the market for a vehicle. And I'm sure your name will come up the next time they get an opportunity to refer you. That is one of many scenarios of great customer service. These are the things great salespeople do to ensure great customer retention.

Value your customers and take care of them. Turn your guests into friends and keep building relationships. Keep thinking of innovative ways to keep your customers coming back to see you. If you have the benefit of working with a company who preaches customer service, take advantage of it. You can express how great your company is to all of your guests on each and every pitch you do. Your guests will feel more comfortable making their purchase with you when they learn about all the great things your company does in order to make their car-buying experience a great one. Then your customers will know that they are getting nothing but the best customer service with you.

## The Inevitable Sales Slump

*"When life gave me lemons, I made the choice to turn them into lemonade."*

There are a lot of ups and downs on the sales floor. You have good days and bad days; sometimes you have more willing customers, and sometimes customers are no not so willing. When faced with bad days and unwilling customers, it's all about how you handle your emotions. Staying positive and energetic and sticking to your sales process is the best advice I can give you.

Any great salesperson will tell you that they have been there. I know I have! I've experienced that feeling when you get caught in the middle of the month, with only a couple of deals down the road, and you wrote a bunch, but they all seem to be unwinding right in front of you, and there is nothing you can do about it. Every opportunity you come across seems to not go your way. You feel like you are not getting good ups. Or you are getting bad leads. You have not gotten a customer to a bill of sale all week, and the weekend is coming up. Your slump is so bad that you are even having trouble closing the door behind you! Well, don't sweat it. It happens to all of us. It's not just you. This kind of slump is just part of the job. It's one of the main reasons why there is a vast amount of turnover in this industry. It's the fear of not making a paycheck that hits you like a ton of bricks when you realize the month is closing in on you faster than you think. You psych yourself out when you start to add up your bills for the month, and then you add your commissions earned and the bills weigh more than your earnings. Let's face it. It's a horrible place to be. And maybe for you it's getting so bad that you are even starting to question whether or not this sales position is for you.

"Maybe I should go work somewhere where I get paid hourly. At least I'll know for sure what my paychecks will look like." **Stop** that thought process! Don't be weak. If you're a salesperson, then go do what salespeople do—that's selling.

The most common mistake made by salespeople who have found their way into that jam is that they start to doubt themselves; they began doubting their ability, and worst of all, doubting their career choice. Don't be pathetic! Like I said, slumps happen. Don't let a bad day or bad week throw you off your game. As a matter of fact, that time should make you stronger and hungrier. It should make you wake up with more determination than you've ever had before. It should set you off; it should make you want to work more hours and talk to more people. You should become relentless when doing your follow-up calls. Stop taking no for an answer, until your month shapes out the way you want it to.

> *Reminder: All it takes is one solid day of selling to turn your month around. My personal best was a five-car day. All sold and rolled. Next time you find yourself in the gutter, just say to yourself, "All I need is one solid day of selling!"*

Another mistake I've seen over and over again is watching a salesperson get in a panic to close a deal. They know that they are behind and that the month's end is creeping up on them. They take every opportunity and pounce on it like a lion in the jungle when it goes in for its next kill. It's like watching a vicious attack. There's no rapport building. The salesperson is very straight to the point: "What can I sell you today?" But this whole "I don't want to know you. I just want to sell you" attitude will never work. The desperation becomes so transparent that the salesperson is dripping sweat balls on the desk trying to close a car deal that he or she is never going to close because the customer is not blind. At this point the customer is thinking one of two things: "Wow, this salesperson is ruthless" or even worse, the customer thinks "Is he on drugs?"

Take it easy; if you are this type of salesperson, you are ruining this business for the rest of us. There's no need to get desperate. Don't embarrass yourself. One of the worst things you can do is panic. Keep your cool and stay calm. If you are too busy focusing on closing the deal, you will forget what it actually takes to close a deal, which is making your customer like you, keeping that customer comfortable with and confident in you, and getting him or her to trust you enough to sign that bill of sale.

In order to sell a car, you need to be able to build a relationship with your customer and earn his or her trust. There is a sales process you need to follow to ensure that you are able to build that relationship with every opportunity you get. Don't get caught in a rush. When you become so focused on closing the deal, you can often start skipping steps in your process. You can become somewhat robotic while talking to your guest to the point that he or she almost forgets you are human. Once you lose that human element, your customer will sense it and not believe you.

The number one thing I believe customers want is to be treated with respect. They want you to be genuine and informative and most importantly professional as you consult them through their car-buying experience. Keep that your main focus. You Be strong enough mentally to not focus on everything that's going wrong for you, and instead keep focusing on everything that's going right. If you go into work every day and know that you are putting forth your best effort, not skipping steps in your process, taking care of all of your guests, and doing everything you can to answer all their questions and help them get what they are asking for, then it's inevitable that you will start closing deals and your month will turn out.

> *Tip: Make yourself a daily reminder of what's most important, and that's your guest experience. Put a Post-it on your desk that reads "How was my guest's experience?" Set a daily reminder on you cell phone. Have it written down on your bedroom dresser or your bathroom mirror. A little reminder like this can make a big impact on what you focus on all day. Try it!*

## Personal Health and Image

> *"Your appearance, attitude, and confidence are what define you as a person."*

> *"When you look like a champ, you'll feel and act like a champ."*

- Energy and Fitness

- Hygiene

- Appearance

There's no better feeling than waking up and getting ready for work, putting on a fresh outfit with a fresh haircut and knowing you look good. You have tons of energy and feel great. You're full of confidence and ready for a full day of interacting with customers. How consistently can you say that you wake up with that state of mind?

### *Energy and Fitness*

Your energy is what will move people and dictate the outcome of every opportunity you receive. The more energy you have, the more effective your performance will be. When was the last time an opportunity walked right by and your split-second reaction was to not talk to them because you felt too lazy to do a deal front to back? The next thing you knew another salesperson grabbed the opportunity and sold those customers a car. Then you thought to yourself, "Damn, that could have been my deal!" It could have, would have, and should have…but it wasn't. You lost that opportunity because you never had enough energy to talk to those customers. You just lost a sale. That's what you get for being a lazy bum!

If you have ever gotten caught in that situation, let's make sure it never happens again. A big part of sales is having enough stamina to go to war for every car deal. Some deals are a battle, and the person with the most endurance wins. You need to be able to outlast your guests. Don't give up. Take your guests on that one extra test drive, boost that extra car, do that one extra presentation. Show your gusts that you are willing to go the extra mile for them and put in the hard work it takes to earn their business until they have nothing left to say but yes.

Where do you find this energy? At the end of the day, it comes down to your personal fitness level. You spend most of your days walking around, burning the rubber of your shoes. You need to be in good shape. The better shape you're in physically, the easier it is for you to maintain a high energy level without burning out.

There are some companies that understand the importance of stay-ing fit, enough so that they actually offer a free gym membership right when you join their team. People tend to respect people who are in good shape. People will respect the fact that you're taking care of your body. And once you have full control of your personal fitness, you will become unstoppable. Not only that, you will gain another level of respect from your guests as well. Believe it or not, people will look up to you for being able to do something that they don't have the willpower to do. Believe me when I say that it takes a lot of willpower to commit to a diet and stay in great shape. By showing your personal commitment to yourself, you are more likely to be looked upon as someone who is fully committed to everything you do. So when you give someone your word, they will be more likely to believe that you will follow through. You will just naturally get a more positive response from people in general.

Car dealing is such a fast-paced environment, and you're always on the go, right? That's the business were in, and it's never going to slow down. Don't get so caught up with making deals happen that you forget about what's most important, and that's your health. Try to avoid fast foods at all costs. Never be too busy to pack a healthy lunch or seek out healthy food choices. It *will* pay off in the long run. The healthier you eat, the healthier you will feel. Keep your body packed with nutritious food choices so that you can perform at the top of your game, day in and day out, and outlast your competition.

Even though it doesn't directly reflect on your day-to-day sales process, taking care of yourself physically is an area in your life that you need to work because it will definitely reflect in how you execute your process on the daily. Maintaining physical fitness is the work outside of work that separates the weak from the obsolete.

*Hygiene*

As a salesperson, you are constantly interacting with other people. As a professional, you need to always make sure you keep up with your personal hygiene. Remember the last time you were dealing with some-one and he or she had bad breath or body odor? It's a very unpleasant situation. It lingers in the back of your mind, and the worse it gets, the harder it becomes for you to concentrate on what you're actually there to do. I know hygiene is a touchy subject, but I feel it's important to men-tion it just as a reminder that it does matter.

To stay professional, always be aware of how your breath smells. This is a big one for cigarette smokers. I'm not here to tell you to quit, although that's a great idea. I'm simply going to remind you that when you go out for a quick smoke and walk back into your dealership, you create an unpleasant aroma that lingers around you for up to an hour, which, coincidentally, is right about the time you're ready for your next smoke. The quickest solution is to always carry a pack of gum or mints on you and have a bottle of cologne at your desk. A lot of guests get offended by smells, enough so that you may lose a deal over it. Same goes for you nonsmokers. A little Juicy Fruit will never hurt anybody.

It's human nature to attract to pleasant smells. When you smell good and your hygiene is in order, people will respect you and want to deal with you. So make sure you are always mindful to maintain a healthy, fresh, and great-smelling body and attitude.

*Appearance*

To play the part, you must dress the part. Salespeople are known to dress in suits and ties or pantsuits and dress shirts. I don't believe you need to wear a suit to sell a car. Although it makes you look professional, you can look just as professional wearing jeans and a polo shirt. Every dealership has its own dress code, so you must dress accordingly. But your professionalism isn't solely dependent on whether you're wearing a suit or not. Professionalism is dependent on how well put together you look and how well you speak. As long as you're dressed appropriately with clean, respectable clothing and you speak well, you will earn credibility with your guests.

Knowledge is power. The more educated you are with what you're doing and the more knowledge you have about your dealership and you're products, the greater salesperson you will be to everyone you talk to. People love to learn, and they love to be educated. Your goal is to be looked upon as the educator, not only by your guests but also by your coworkers. Once you've set that standard for yourself and you're looked at as a role model, you will demand a different level of respect that, in return, will attract more people to you in a positive way.

Whether you're attracting new customers or people you work with, the main thing is that you're attracting positivity. When you can grasp that last statement and understand the upside to it, you are on your way to becoming a true leader. To be the best at what you do, you must have a burning desire to lead. To be a true powerhouse performer, you need to have a great work ethic and the will to manage your own business and network your way to the top.

# Chapter 2:
# The Seven Steps of Selling

In this chapter, we'll discuss the seven steps of selling that I've devised. Step one is Attitude, which was discussed in depth in Chapter 1, so we'll begin this chapter by discussing the second step, meet and greet.

1. Attitude

2. Meet and Greet

3. Investigate/Qualify

4. Presentation

5. Demonstration

6. Close

7. Follow-up

# Meet and Greet

*"You never get a second chance to make a first impression."*

It all starts here. The way you introduce yourself to your guest sets the tone for your sale. Are you smiling, happy, excited, and full of energy? Or are you monotone, nervous, timid, and scared to shake somebody's hand? You need to be personable if you're trying to make a great first impression. There will be people who are very receptive to you right from the get-go, and there will be others who you're going to have to win over with your charisma.

When you meet a customer for the first time, how do you want to come across? Of course you want to come off as professional and friendly. You want your guests to feel comfortable with you so that you can earn their trust and their business.

When you think of a standard meet and greet, what comes to mind?

*Salesperson*: "Hey, welcome to the dealership. My name is Derek, and you are?"

*Customer*: "Hey, I'm Brad."

*Salesperson*: "Hey, Brad. How are you doing? Are you here to see anyone in particular?"

*Customer*: "No. This is my first time in the store."

*Salesperson*: "Perfect. I'll be happy to help you out. Come on over to my desk so we can get started."

*Boring*, right? That is such a typical and mediocre way to introduce oneself, and we have all been doing it that way for years. But we are living in the twenty-first century now. I think it's time we spiced that meet and greet up a bit. Don't get me wrong. The standard meet and greet is what it is for a reason. It allows you to identify if the customer you are talking to is already dealing with another associate or if he or she is fair game for you to start your selling process. You still need to find out if the guest that you're introducing yourself to already has an appointment with another salesperson. The last thing you want to do is deal with one of your associate's guests. That's a good way to start friction between the two of you. Also, it's a good idea to find out if the guest has ever been to the dealership prior to your encounter. If he or she has, there's a good chance that you can pull up his or her information through the dealership's database. By doing so, you can find information about the guest that could become useful to you throughout your deal, such as previous purchases or previous credit information.

Let's think outside the box, though, and start making a big impact on initial introductions. Your goal should be to be a little more dynamic than the next guy. That's what will get you from being good to being great. Think of some different ways to do a cool meet and greet, and then try them out. I guarantee you that your guests will appreciate it. I'll get you started with a couple of examples:

> *Salesperson*: "Hey, guys! You must be Maria and James. You guys decided to come visit me early. That's great! How are you doing today?"

> *Customer*: "We are doing fine, thank you, but our names are Amanda and Jeromy."

> *Salesperson*: "Oh really? How embarrassing! I do apologize. I thought you may have been this sweet couple I've been waiting for. I have them booked in for tomorrow, but they said they may come surprise me earlier."

> *Customer*: "No, we don't actually have an appointment booked with anyone. We just had a couple of questions about some of your vehicles."

> *Salesperson*: "OK. Awesome. Since I have your attention, I'd be more than happy to help you guys out. Come on over."

The example above demonstrates a good way to get customer names. Also you come across as humble, busy, and enthusiastic right from the get-go. Those are all great qualities for a salesperson to have.

In the next example, let's say a couple walks in with their child:

*Salesperson*: "Hey, guys! Welcome to the dealership. My name is Derek, and you are?"

*Customer 1*: "Erica."

*Salesperson*: "And you are?"

*Customer 2*: "Adam."

*Salesperson*: "And this must be Canada's next top model because she's so adorable!"

*Customer 1*: "Oh, thank you. Her name is Violet."

*Salesperson*: "She's too cute. What an angel! Were you guys here to see anyone today, or did you want me to help you out?"

*Customer 2*: "No, you can help us out for sure."

*Salesperson*: "Awesome. Let's go to my desk so we can get started!"

One thing parents can never get enough of is compliments about their children. By opening with a meet and greet like that, you can win some points early on in the game.

Putting a little extra flavor in your meet and greet will go a long way. It shows that you have character. People like to experience things out of the ordinary, within reason, of course. It's the little things like a great opening that will differentiate you from your competitors. It will also make you memorable in a good way down the road come time for referrals.

*I'm just looking....*

If I had a dollar for every time I heard "I'm just looking" come out of a customer's mouth…

That is a classic reflex objection commonly used by customers who are truly just looking and want to find a vehicle on your lot that piques their interest. Don't let that response intimidate you. Don't take it as an objection. Use it as an opening for you to start the sales process. When a customer says "I'm just looking," this means he or she is looking to buy but hasn't quite found what he or she is looking for yet. So if a customer is just looking, that's OK. Just make sure you stay close by and help him or her look. That way you can be the one to help him or her out with a purchase once he or she finds a vehicle.

I have a few lines you can put in your toolbox for the next time you hear the classic line "I'm just looking":

"Perfect, and what are you looking for?"

"Are you looking for anything in particular?"

"Awesome! Let me help you. I got a million dollars in inventory on the lot. I can't let you look alone, ha-ha."

"Great! Are you looking for a car, truck, SUV, minivan, or crossover?"

"Fantastic! I'll look with you just in case you have any questions. I'll be right here to answer them."

"Oh, really? How long have you been looking for?"

"Looking to buy?"

Practice those lines, and at the same time brainstorm a couple of your own. You can never have enough. There should be no reason to ever hit another roadblock when someone says "I'm just looking." That classic line will become your new segue into your next car deal.

*I just wanted to get the price of that vehicle...*

Yes, ladies and gentlemen, this is another classic line most commonly heard from buyers. Price, price, price, price! They always want to know the price first. Fair enough; they are fully entitled to get the price. These days most prices are listed online anyway. Don't be the salesperson who tries to deflect the price and goes into another subject. If someone wants a price, you need to tell them the price. We have nothing to hide. The customer is going to find out the price eventually, and he or she may even know it already. The key for you is to be able to give the customer the price and then go back and take control of the sale and find out what really matters. Find out what a customer's price range is and find out exactly what he or she is looking to buy. Start investigating and qualifying things like budget and vehicles of interest. I'll get more into that in my next section.

You need to be able to give someone a price and pull them back in by asking questions and having answers. To be a great salesperson, you need to be full of ammunition. Always be ready to ask a question, and always be ready to give an answer. Here are some questions and answers I use on someone when they ask me "What's the price?"

"The price is...Were you looking to find something in a particular price range?"

"That specific vehicle is listed in and around the twenty-thousand-dollar range. Let's go inside so I can get you an exact answer."

"What price range are you looking to be in?"

"That vehicle is priced accordingly in the market. Are you after that car specifically, or were you looking for something in a certain price range?"

"I'm not sure. Let's go over to my office so I can get that answer for you."

"What would you like it to be?"

"We have a twenty-four-hour pricing system here. Let's go find out today's market price."

"For a nice fellow like you, I'll make sure you get a great deal."

"You tell me what you think the price is, and I'll tell you how close you are!"

These are all great responses to use the next time you are asked the phantom question "What's your price?" As long as you're quick to respond, it's OK if you have a little fun with your answers. You will be dealing with many different personalities, however, so make sure your response matches the vibes you're getting from your guest. There's a right response for every guest. You need to determine which response goes with which guest. Your timing is key.

> *Reminder: The only way to get people in a buying mood is to win them over with your character. If they like you, they will buy from you.*

Your initial encounter with anyone should always be positive. You need to go into every hand shake, every smile, and every exchange of names with a great attitude. Be enthusiastic every time you speak. Make every word count. You will be talking to a lot of customers throughout your time on the sales floor, so don't be afraid to try new things and see what works best for you. Your meet and greet is only the beginning of your sales process, but it will set the tone for the entire sale. Use it to your advantage. Make a great first impression every time; that way you will create a great customer experience right from the get-go, and it will be easier for you to guide your guests through the next steps.

# Investigate/Qualify

*"In order to navigate, you must communicate."*

*"Your guest sheet should be to you what Picasso's canvas was to him."*

Most dealerships have a system now where it is mandatory for a sales-person to fill out a guest sheet with his or her guest within five minutes of the initial encounter. If you work for a dealership that isn't doing this, I strongly advise that you start this process. Your guest sheet is everything. It gives you the opportunity to build a relationship with your guest, qualify your guest, investigate why your guest is in the market for a vehicle, and most importantly help you navigate your way into a car deal.

Everything we discuss in regards to investigating and qualifying should be done while filling out a guest sheet. Having a guest sheet gives you the opportunity to sit your guest down and explain to him or her what the guest sheet's purpose is.

A guest sheet is designed to allow you to find out exactly what it is your guest is looking for. It allows you to find out if your guest is trading in a vehicle. If so, it allows you to find out if your guest has an existing lien on that vehicle. If so, by finding out the guest's existing lien, you can determine whether or not your guest will have any negative equity. The reason why that information is so important is that depending on the amount of negative equity a guest has, he or she may not be able to look at vehicles of a certain age; also, negative equity will reflect on a guest's new monthly payment due to the extra amount of cash being carried over. Make sure you factor a guest's negative equity into the equation before you select a vehicle to demonstrate.

> *Reminder: There will be times where trade-in value will make or break your car deal. There is a devalue process you can go through during your trade appraisal. Trade-in values should always be determined at the end of the sale, never the beginning.*

Guest sheets are also used to discuss monthly budgets. They give you an opportunity to see how flexible someone's monthly budget is. The information provided will let you know whether or not your guest is firm on his or her monthly budget or if he or she has some room to play with. That information, in turn, will help you when you are out selecting a vehicle for the guest. If you have a guest who is firm on his or her budget, you are going to have a hard time trying to bump him or her on payments, so make sure to select a vehicle that you know you can make work within his or her budget.

Guest sheets also give you an opportunity to find out what your guests' hot buttons are. What are their favorite colors, and what features would they really love to have in their new vehicle? The more features and hot buttons you can find for them, and still be in their monthly budget, the more likely they are to say yes to you when you ask for the sale. If you fill out a guest sheet properly, you should be able to determine whether or not you got a car deal, and if so, how difficult of a deal it will be.

## *Investigate*

You have reached a very important step. Once you get past your meet and greet, you ultimately want to get your guests to sit down with you at your desk so you can start investigating, and by investigating, what I really mean is digging a little deeper by asking questions and finding out what brought your guest away from his or her everyday life and into your dealership to purchase a vehicle. What's the guest's motive? What did he or she come to accomplish?

The stronger a salesperson you are, the smoother you will be while trying to collect all this information from your guest. You can just ask point-blank question after question until you have a full guest sheet filled out. Some people may not be so receptive to that, however. There's no fun involved. The proper way to gather guest sheet information is through conversation. Your ability to engage yourself in a conversation with a guest and throughout your conversation slip in a question here and there that will help you find the guest's buying motive is what will set you apart from the average salesperson. A lot of sales are lost in this specific step in the sales process. Without realizing it, there are salespeople out there who have a lack of relationship-building and communication skills. This is an area we need to focus on so we don't lose a sale before it even starts.

> *Tip: The key to successful investigation is being able to ask the right questions at the right time. The more questions you have to ask, the better.*

How do you build a relationship with your guest? It's really not that hard. Remember, you're not trying to become best friends for life with everyone. You are simply trying to create a good business relationship. You want to be perceived as friendly, professional, and someone who genuinely has his or her guest's best interest in mind. You want to build a formal relationship with your guests. Your goal is to become their car guy or gal. In return, you offer them nothing but the best customer service possible.

So how can you kick-start a conversation? Start asking more questions! I'm going to give you some conversation starters to help you get on your way. As you read my starts, I want you to think up some of your own. The more you have, the better!

"How long have you been in Edmonton for?"

"Where did you guys grow up?"

"How long have you been in that line of work?"

"Where did you go to school? What university did you study at?"

"What brought you guys in today?"

"What are you currently driving?"

"Why are you looking to upgrade today?"

"What do you guys do for fun?"

"What features are most important to you and your family?"

"How will this vehicle mainly be used in your everyday life?"

Try using some of these lines the next time you try to kick-start a conversation with a guest. Watch how fast the relationship building starts. After a few minutes of conversation, you should be able to get your guest's guard down. Another key thing to wait for is an opportunity within your conversation to find a common ground. It could be that you guys both grew up in the same town or both went to the same school. It could be that you are both fans of a certain sports club, or you both have a mutual friend. It's a small world. You would be surprised how often you can find common ground. It's just a matter of paying attention and looking for it. Once you find common ground, use it to your advantage. The goal is to be perceived as a friend and not a stranger. By finding that common ground, your guest will see you as not so much of a stranger as he or she did when you initially introduced yourself. Once you've opened that door, you're on your way to the qualifying process.

*Qualify*

Qualifying your guests is done for several reasons. First, you want to confirm that they are eligible for financing. Depending on what kind of dealership you work at, your store will attract a certain type of customer. Some stores attract more prime customers, and other stores attract more subprime customers. It's always important to know the financial situation of your guests. When they tell you they want to finance, essentially what they are doing is looking to apply for a bank loan. Having that in mind and taking that approach, there should be no reason why your guests will have any issue with giving you their credit information. The people who are most willing to give you their personal information without any hesitation will usually be the ones with bad credit history. People with bad credit history are aware that they have credit issues. They will be more concerned with the amount they can get financed for and what kind of interest rates they will be paying. When you are dealing with a guest in that situation, it's always a good idea to take the credit specialist route. Start the financing process. See what kind of approval your finance team can generate for the guest, and select a vehicle accordingly. Your goal will be to get your guest into a vehicle as close to the vehicle he or she initially desired.

On the other hand, there will be some guests who will not give you any of their personal information other than their name and phone number until you have provided them with a vehicle that they are excited to buy. Those guys will usually tell you that they have no credit issues and that they are not concerned about being approved for financing. In those situations, use your better judgment and take the guest's word for it. Don't insist on getting his or her information right from the get-go. That's a good way to make your guest feel like he or she is being pushed into a sale, and once you put yourself in that corner it's hard to get yourself out. Don't get caught fulfilling this stereotype. Don't be pushy. If you ask for your guest's personal credit information and your guest is uncomfortable giving it to you, it's OK. That just means you have not won him or her over yet. You need to default back to your sales process and wait for another opportunity to request the information. The next time you go for the credit information should be right after the guest has chosen a vehicle that he or she is happy to buy. Before you start working out monthly payments is a great time to tell your guest that you need his or her credit information to get more accurate monthly payments. Remember, every guest is going to be different. Some people are going to be open and willing to give you everything you ask for, and then there are others who are going to be more guarded throughout the sales process. It's part of the game. You have to deal with everyone on a case-by-case basis.

Another great reason for qualifying your guest is to determine what stage of the buying process he or she is in. When you're dealing with customers in this industry, there are always different motives and personalities that you will discover. You will run into impulse buyers and nonimpulse buyers. You will also run into people who are all in different buying stages.

I've narrowed these stages down to three. There's the beginning stage, where guests put their buying plan into motion. Then you have the middle stage, where you will find guests caught between decisions. And then there is the final stage. The final stage is where the guest pulls the trigger and jumps into the closing phase. The people in the beginning stage usually start out by going online and researching vehicles of interest in their desired price point. They will find a couple vehicles they like at a couple different dealerships and set aside a day to go out and actually view these vehicles. Once they have been out to a couple different dealers to test drive some vehicles to see what vehicle they like the best they enter the middle stage. The final stage is reached when they have done all of their research, have driven a couple different makes and models, and are ready to make a decision and talk to someone about financing options. As a power performer, you want to be able to identify what stage your guests are in and guide them through the rest of their decision-making process to make sure your product reins dominant over the competitors' products.

> *Tip: Many guests can go from the beginning stage to the final stage all in one day, so make sure you try to close the deal **now**!*

This guideline I'm giving you applies to the majority of guests, but not to all. It's your job to determine what type of guest you have sitting in front of you. Try out some of these qualifying questions the next time you're trying to navigate your way to a car deal:

*"Are you currently financing anything?"*

You want to know if your guest has any current loans out. It gives you an idea of how much money they are currently borrowing from the banks.

This is good information to know if the guest is looking for another loan. Customers will only be able to acquire a certain amount of money depending on their income. So if they already have multiple loans, it may be difficult for them to acquire another.

*"Are you financing your current vehicle?"*

It's very important to find out if your guest's current vehicle is being financed, especially if he or she is planning on trading it. You need to find out what the existing lien is, as well as all the specifications on the vehicle. The more seasoned you are in the car business, the easier it will be for you to determine if you're dealing with a negative equity situation and just how much negative equity there is. Depending on the amount of negative equity your guest has, you may run into a situation where there is too much money to carry over, or monthly payments can go way over budget once you add in the negative equity.

*"What lending institution is financing that for you?"*

By finding out which bank is financing your guest's current vehicle will give you a really good idea as to what kind of credit situation he or she is in. All banks have different financing options. Some banks will only lend at prime interest rates, so someone applying for a loan needs to have good, established credit in order to qualify. Then there are other banks that specialize in financing at subprime interest rates for people who have poor credit history. Knowing this information will help you take the proper approach with every guest.

*"Do you have any credit cards?"*

Find out if your guest has any credit cards. This question is good for the younger guys between eighteen and twenty-five years old. Credit cards are a great way to start establishing credit. If you have a young buyer looking to finance, this question is a great way to find out if he or she has any established credit. On the other hand, if you are dealing with someone a little bit older who says he or she doesn't have any credit cards, that information should usually raise a red flag. Someone could not have credit cards because he or she couldn't keep up with payments and had the cards canceled by credit grantors. Another good reason to ask this question is so when you ask a guest if he or she has any credit cards and the answer is yes, then the guest can tell you his or her credit card balance as well. It's going to be easier for you to get a deposit at the end of your sale because you know as well as your guest knows, based on what he or she has told you, that he or she is capable of leaving a deposit. Don't ever put your guests on the spot if they tell you they can't afford leave a deposit even though you know they have lots of room on their credit cards. It's misusing their personal information, and some guests will get offended. Use the information to your advantage. If guests tell you they can't leave a deposit and you know they have room on their credit card, then they must have an objection to some part of the deal that you're offering that's holding them back. Take a moment and try to find out what that objection is.

*"What's your monthly budget for your new vehicle?"*

Don't make the mistake of not asking this question. Budget, budget, budget! A majority of our society lives on a monthly budget. When you are dealing with a guest, find out what his or her budget is. You need to be able to find out a comfortable monthly budget and see if there is any flexibility. Spend a couple minutes talking to your guest about his or her budget and find out why that budget is what it is and how your guest generated it. Once you have a good idea of how tight or flexible the budget is, you can advance to the next step in your process, which is landing your guest on a vehicle that he or she is happy to purchase. You need to be able to guide them toward a vehicle that will fit within his or her monthly budget. A rookie mistake is showing your guest a vehicle that you know will not line up with his or her monthly budget. Don't shoot yourself in the foot. If you make that mistake and try to show your guest a payment that is substantially higher than the payment he or she told you was comfortable, you will lose all credibility, and your guest will start to see the dollar signs in your eyes. Listen to the budget first, and then locate a vehicle accordingly. If you are still new to the business and don't have an idea of what vehicles to show, get your manager involved. He or she will be able to guide you toward the right vehicles.

*"What changed in your driving needs that brought you into the store today?"*

This question is a great conversation starter. Asking this question opens the door for your guest to let you know exactly what it is he or she is looking for in a vehicle. It also gives the guest an opportunity to explain to you why he or she is at your dealership. That will give you an idea of the guest's current driving situation, and then you will know how urgent or not so urgent buying a car is for him or her.

*"Where are you currently working?"*

Make sure to find out if your guest is currently employed. It doesn't matter if a guest has good credit or bad credit. Without any provable income, he or she will not qualify for any type of loan. There are a lot of lending institutions, typically subprime lending institutions, that have a three-month probation period before someone is eligible for a car loan. Look out for waitresses and bartenders. These types of laborers typically make the lump sum of their monthly income in tips. In most cases, these tips are not claimed. Their provable income is usually lower than the minimum requirements set by the financial institutions. So make sure when these guests tell you their monthly income you separate their tips from their actual taxed income. Another group to look out for is private contractors. People who are self-employed or subcontracting will usually need to provide T4s or notice of assessments for two-plus years, depending on the length of time they have been self-employed and depending on their credit. Your finance team may have a hard time getting income conformation from the banks, again depending on what kind of credit history your guest has.

*"Were you planning on putting down an initial investment?"*

Find out how comfortable and flexible your guest is with putting down an initial investment. You may be able to expand your vehicle search if your guest is comfortable putting money down. The more money that a guest can put down, the lower his or her monthly payment will be. This will allow you to maximize on gross potential in your car deal.

*"What's your gross income?"*

Find out how much money your guest makes per month. There is a minimum amount required to qualify for a loan, usually around $1600–1800 per month. This amount will vary from bank to bank. Also lending institutions only allow a certain monthly payment based on your guest's income. Keep that in mind when you are discussing payments with your guest.

*"How soon are you looking to make a purchase?"*

This is a great question to ask to get a good idea of what buying stage your guest is in—if he or she is looking to buy now, if he or she is just starting out, if he or she has been looking for six months. Also, you will get a good idea as to whether your guest is an impulse buyer or nonimpulse buyer. The people who are looking to buy now are the best type of guests. They don't want to shop around; they just want to get a good car for a good deal so that they can get back to their everyday life. The people who are just starting out can go both ways. Some of them will buy right when they find what they want, while others will shop a few different dealers to try and get the best bang for their buck. Then you have the people who have been shopping for six months or longer. Well, that pretty much says it all. It doesn't take six or more months to find a vehicle, I guarantee you that. When you run across guests like this, you will want to question why they have been looking for so long. Cut to the chase quick, or you may find yourself following up with these guys for the next six months.

**Reminder: Just because a guest tells you that he or she is not buying today, that may not be the case.** What the guest really means is "I'm not buying yet because I have not found what I am looking for." As a seasoned salesperson, you still have to ask for the sale. If you asked twice and you feel like you're starting to come as across as pushy, you probably are, and that's OK. Let the guest leave with a good taste in his or her mouth. Follow up with the guest twenty minutes later with a text that looks something like this: "Hey, guys! Thanks for the opportunity today to earn your business. It was a pleasure meeting you. I look forward to hearing from you guys tomorrow. Have a great night, and God bless!"

A nice text like that should really touch those guests who are genuinely interested in your product. It's out of the norm, and shows just a little extra character on your part. The people who are serious will usually be the ones who respond to the text. The ones who don't respond typically will never step foot in your dealership again. You still need to follow up with everyone, however. This will just tell you who is worth the most in following up.

**Expand your inventory.** When you are talking to your guest about what type of vehicles he or she is interested in, always dig a little deeper into his or her answers. If a guest tells you that he or she is looking for a truck, find out why the guest needs a truck. Also ask your guest if he or she would be open to SUVs, vans, or crossovers. The same deal applies when a guest tells you that he or she wants a Ford. No problem. What is it about Ford that your guest likes, and also would he or she be open to looking at different makes? By asking your guest if he or she is open to different makes and models, you're allowing yourself the opportunity to show him or her more vehicles. This gives you better odds at landing them on a vehicle to purchase.

**Never judge a book by its cover**. The one thing I can never understand is how a salesperson can prequalify a guest based on his or her appearance without even sitting down and having a conversation with the guest or asking some qualifying questions and investigating. Never be too good for your own good. To be a powerhouse, you always need to go back to basics. The basic steps are what will get you to become a top performer. Don't take shortcuts, and don't ever not sit down and talk to a guest because you decided to prejudge him or her. Every opportunity counts in this business. Don't miss out on any. Talk to everyone you possibly can, and see how you can muster up a deal.

Once you have mastered the qualifying process, the last steps in the sales process become a breeze. Keep your energy level high, and make sure you make the buying process exciting for your guests.

## Presentation

Presenting a vehicle—it's the best part of this job. This is when it's really show time. This is the point of sale where your main focus is getting your guest so excited about the vehicle that he or she can't wait to test drive it. The more exciting and educational your presentation is, the more likely your guest is to buy the car. Your attitude toward your product needs to be like no other. You need to talk about all the exciting new features as if they were the most innovative, mind-blasting features your guest will ever see in his or her lifetime.

By this this point in your process, you already have a good idea of what your guest is looking for. If you are selling new vehicles, you have already talked about what makes and models your guest would like to look at that are in line with his or her budget. Now it's time to get your guest in front of a vehicle and excite them.

The best way to present a vehicle is to pull it up to the front of the dealership. Isolate it from all the other vehicles on the lot. That way when you are doing your vehicle walk-around with your guest and you are showing them all the features and gadgets the vehicle comes equipped with, your guest's attention will stay on the vehicle at hand as opposed to all the other vehicles you took out of eyesight. Not only that, by isolating the vehicle from the other vehicles, you allow yourself and your guests enough space to walk around the outside of the vehicle so that you all can get to view the vehicle comfortably from all angles. One of the biggest mistakes you can do is show a vehicle while it is still in the vehicle lineup. You can't do a proper walk-around. Your guest can barely open the doors without hitting the next car. You are denying your guest the opportunity to really appreciate the vehicle, and you are also denying yourself the opportunity to build value in the vehicle. You will make this step in the process very unpleasant, and in return, your guest's emotions may go from feeling good to feeling bad. Don't give your guest a reason to have any negative feedback about you or your dealership. Be a professional and do it right.

> *Reminder: Buyers buy based on emotion. The start of the presentation process is the start of the emotional incline for every guest. This step is where the guest really starts to get excited about his or her vehicle purchase. He or she starts to visualize actually owning that new piece of shiny metal!*

*Building Value*

Don't miss the opportunity to build value in your product. If your guest cannot see the value, he or she will not pay for your product. Never take your competitors for granted. Whatever makes and models you're selling, there will always be a competitor next door selling comparable makes and models. Do your research and find out what makes your product dominant over all the others.

Make sure to express to your guest during every presentation what your vehicles have to offer that other vehicles don't, and more importantly, how your guest will benefit from what your vehicles offer. It's easy to name off all the new features a vehicle has to offer. All you need to do is study the brochure. But the most effective way to build value in these features is to follow them up by explaining how your guest can use these features and benefit from them in their everyday life.

> *Example 1*: This vehicle has Bluetooth. This vehicle comes equipped with a hands-free Bluetooth system that will automatically connect to your cell phone the second you get inside your vehicle. This way you can talk on the phone while driving and still keep your hands at ten and two. Having this feature will keep you from being distracted on the roads for a safe ride home every time. Also, with the new laws across the province, it is now illegal drive while using a cell phone.

> *Example 2*: This vehicle comes with park-assist censors. This vehicle comes equipped with censors that will actually notify you via alert tones if you are getting too close to a curb or if you are getting too close to another vehicle. The closer you get, the louder and faster the alert tones will become. This is a good feature to have if you are parking in a tight space or if you are trying to parallel park. This

feature will eliminate your risk of scratching up your tires and bumpers. You wouldn't want to scratch up such a beautiful vehicle like this!

*Example 3*: This vehicle has child safety locks. This vehicle has a great safety feature installed in the rear doors to protect your children. If you open the rear door, there is a safety switch you can hit that will not allow the rear doors to be opened from the inside of the vehicle. They can only be opened from the outside. This way when you have your kids in the back seat, you will have no worries about them playing with the buttons and accidentally opening the car doors while you are driving. It's just another safety feature that ensures a safe ride every time. Let me show you how they work.

*Example 4*: This vehicle has touchscreen audio and navigation. Hop inside the car. I'm going to show you how the touchscreen audio and navigation system works. This feature gives you the best of both worlds. Not only do you get the touchscreen audio control that helps you control the AM/FM CD player. It also controls the navigation system to ensure you never get lost. It's a great feature to have if you're planning on taking any road trips into uncharted territory.

*Example 5*: This vehicle has a rear DVD player. This vehicle comes equipped with a rear DVD player for the children. This is a great feature to have if you want to keep the kids busy while on the road. By having the luxury of a rear DVD player, you can keep your children's attention on a movie or television show while you safely drive from point A to point B without screaming children to distract you. Let me go grab a DVD so I can show you how to operate it. (Go the extra mile and give your guest a quick tutorial on how to operate the DVD player. You will earn extra points with your guest. Also by doing so, it will separate you from the average salesperson.)

Selling used vehicles is more or less the same. When you are selling used vehicles, you need to remember that financing options may vary depending on the year of and kilometers on the vehicle you are looking to sell. There are more variables involved when you are trying to match up a vehicle of interest and monthly budget at the same time.

> *Reminder: The older the vehicle and the higher the kilometers, the less amount of time the lending institutions will allow you to borrow money.*

How can you help your guest land a vehicle if that guest is not sure about what he or she wants? Use the process of elimination method. First, narrow down your search from car, truck, SUV, crossover, or minivan. Once you guys have decided that it's either going to be one or the other, get out on the lot and wait for something to jump out at your guest. Depending on how much inventory you're packed with, your guest will more than likely land himself or herself on a couple of vehicles that he or she finds interesting.

It's now up to you to advance in your opportunity to grab the keys so you can go into your vehicle presentation. You want to excite your guest enough on the presentation that he or she wants to go for a test drive. After the test drive, if you still can't get verbal commitment from your guest to own the vehicle and he or she insists on looking at others, no worries. It happens. Try to help your guest narrow the choice down, and tell him or her, "Perfect! What we're going to do is pick out two more vehicles for you to view and test drive. After we do that, you can decide between the two which one you are going to go with!" If you say that to your guest and he or she agrees, then he or she just verbally agreed to decide between two more vehicles. That just tells you that you are one step closer to a car deal. If the guest disagrees with you and tells you he or she will not be deciding today, that's OK too. That just means you are dealing with a nonimpulse buyer, and he or she needs more time, or it could mean that you still have not impressed that particular guest enough for him or her to give you a commitment to purchase from you. That's all the more reason for you to keep a great attitude and find those hot buttons.

# Demonstration

The demonstration is the first time your guest gets to hop inside a vehicle with you and go for a test drive. This is another huge step in the selling process. The test drive is mandatory in my neck of the woods. If someone doesn't drive it, he or she doesn't buy it, especially if you are selling a used car. If you are selling new cars, you may be able to get away with demonstrating the same vehicle that a customer wants to buy but in a different color. That's understandable if the customer's preferred color is a vehicle that needs to be located. For the most part, you don't want to miss this opportunity to allow your guest to get behind the wheel of his or her new vehicle and enjoy that first road test. Again, you need to remember that this is the point of sale where your guests are on an emotional high. They start to picture themselves driving that car every day, and they start to think how great it would feel to own a new car. This is where all their emotions are buzzing, and they are more inclined to say yes to you based on their desire to own the car.

Let me tell you what to look for during your test drive. You need to be aware of buying signals. This is where you are going to have to read your guests' body language as well as their verbal language. A test drive is going to go one of two ways. If your test drive is going well, you will start to hear your guest say things like "Hey, this is really comfortable" or "I like how there is so much room in the front seat" or "This vehicle drives really nice."

Those are all positive statements about the vehicle. The more positive statements your guest makes on a test drive and the more you see him or her smiling from how happy he or she is to be driving the vehicle, the more likely your guest is to say yes to you when you ask him or her the magic question. The magic question to ask every guest after every test drive is "So, Mr. Customer, if I can make the numbers work and make this vehicle totally affordable and feasible within your budget, would you take it home right now?" When your guest says yes, you are one step closer to closing your car deal. What you just got is verbal commitment to purchase a vehicle that you just landed on. That is your cue to go back into the dealership and start the closing process on paper.

In a perfect world, that's how every test drive would go. Well, let me tell you, it's not that easy, people. If it were that easy to sell a car, we wouldn't see the amount of turnover we do in the industry. You need to be able to get rejected and not flinch. You need to be able to hear the word *no* and say, "Why not?" As a top performer, you need to find out why your guest is saying no and what you need to do to turn that no into a yes. What's the objection? What are you missing? Is it the car? Is it the price? Is it the payment? Are all the decision makers present? Is it your insurance quote? Do you need to drive one more vehicle just to compare your options? How can I seal the deal? Sometimes it's a battle, and the person who comes out on top is the person with the most determination. You need to mentally train yourself to look at every opportunity as a car deal. If you've mentally checked yourself out of a deal and you've told yourself that these guests aren't buying today, then guess what? They *are* buying, just not from you. How can you sell a car to someone if you already put the idea in your head that he or she isn't buying? You're too busy thinking about how you're going to blow them out of the dealership rather than how you can navigate your way into a car deal.

Now, the other way your test drive can go is like this. You get inside the vehicle, and your guest starts driving, and you start to hear things like "Oh, that doesn't feel right" or "I can't really see anything from the rearview mirror" or "Hmmm…I wonder what else you guys have on the lot."

Those are all negative statements about the vehicle. If those kinds of negative statements are made on your test drive, you can still ask the magic question after the test drive, but you're more likely to hear the answer no. In this situation it's always to best to go back a step and go land your guest on a different vehicle. Don't try to close your guests on a vehicle if you know that they weren't all that excited about it. All that does is make you look pushy. You will lose credibility if you don't go the extra mile and find them a vehicle they are excited to own. If you try to close your guest on a vehicle that he or she wasn't too happy about, then all you're going to do is set yourself up for them to walk out on you or start making up excuses on how they have to leave right away.

Be a champion and take some pride in what you do. Make an extra effort to ensure that your guest is happy and committed to buying your vehicle. In this business, it's all about customer service. The extra efforts you make are the ones that will make you memorable.

Make sure you get the right commitment. Learn how to handle objections. If a guest tells you that he or she liked the vehicle, but the only thing he or she wasn't happy with was the fact that it didn't have A/C, then your response should be "Other than the fact that the vehicle doesn't have A/C, is there any other reason why we couldn't wrap this up right now?" If your guest says no, then you can proceed back into the dealership and start working out payment options. Another good question to ask is "Is A/C a deal breaker for you?" If the guest says yes, then stop right there and go find a vehicle with A/C. If you fill out a proper guest sheet prior to selecting a vehicle, you will not run into these issues because you will have already discussed hot buttons and must-have options at this time.

If a guest tells you that he or she loves the vehicle but it needs two new front tires, then go for the kill. Ask him or her "So what you're saying is if I can talk to my manager and get you two new front tires installed, you will be happy enough to own this vehicle right now?" If your guest says yes, then *bang!* You just got a car deal. There's no manager out there who would walk a deal over two tires. He or she may try to split the cost with your guest, and you can't blame him or her for that. After all, it is your manager's job to hold gross.

It's a different scenario if your guest tells you that he or she will purchase the vehicle, but his or her wish list is a page long, starting with tires, car starter, removing the scratches, removing the smoke smell from the vehicle, and all the way to installing aftermarket cruise control. At this point, it's safe to say that you have landed on the wrong vehicle! Tell your guest that you don't think the vehicle is right for him or her, and then go back a step and land the guest on another vehicle that interests him or her without all the obstacles.

# Close

> *"If I can make the numbers work and make this purchase totally affordable and feasible, is this vehicle the right vehicle for you?"*

OK, all you salespeople. This is what we live for—the rush of the close. After all your hard work going from step one to step five, you have now finally worked your way to step six, the negotiation process. This is where the real fun begins! This is the step where you start discussing payment options and deposits and getting full commitment to purchasing your product.

There are multiple ways to close a deal, from the old-school Benjamin Franklin close all the way to looking at the pros and cons of making this purchase. All are very cool and very fun closes. I personally believe that customers have evolved with the help of the information they can research on the Internet, and they are now more aware of their budget and have educated themselves about the product and their financing options well before they step foot into a dealership. This isn't a bad thing; it just means that have to be just as educated as they are and then some so that when they ask you questions you can give them the right answers. The worst thing that can happen is having a guest who knows more about your product and financing options than you do. Stay sharp and in tune with what's going on at your dealership!

The number one rule you need to follow if you are going to be a successful closer is that if you properly take a guest from step one, which is a great attitude, all the way through to step six, which is the close (negotiation process), without taking any shortcuts and by handling objections as they come to you, you should have properly set up your deal so that the only answer that comes out of your guest's mouth is yes.

Remember: Step one of your sales success is your great attitude. Your attitude will be your driving force throughout the entire sale. Even if you're getting frustrated in dealing with a tougher guest, don't let your attitude deteriorate. Stay positive and energetic the whole way through!

I'm going to show you how to set up your deal so that when you get to the negotiation process, the close, you line it up so well that you don't even give your guest the option of saying no. In fact, the only thing that they can tell you is yes.

In order to get full commitment on purchasing a vehicle, you need to have three things in place:

1. All the decision makers have to be present.

2.   Your guest needs to have the vehicle presented to them, and they also need to have taken the vehicle for a road test (test drive).

3.   Your guest needs to be verbally committed to purchasing the vehicle.

The best time to clarify if all the decision makers are present is right at the beginning of your deal while you are filling out a guest sheet. This will allow you to properly line up your deal to know when to go into the negotiation stage. You never want to go to paper and try to close a guest on numbers if all the decision makers aren't present. If you do, you are leaving your guest with an out. If you know that all the decision makers aren't present and you go to paper, your guest has the option to tell you that he or she needs to go talk to a partner or whoever it is that isn't present at the moment who would need to be present in order for the guest to pull the trigger and buy the car. Not only are you giving them an out, the guest now knows what monthly payments you are offering, which gives him or her the opportunity to go to the next dealership to see if that dealership will beat your numbers. Don't put yourself in that situation. If you find out right from the get-go that all decision makers are not present, then don't go into the negotiation process. Go as far as step five (test drive), and at that point your goal should be to book an appointment for as soon as possible to get the final decision maker into the dealership so that you can start your close.

Presenting the vehicle to your guest and making sure he or she test drives it is another must before starting the closing process. By presenting the vehicle to your guest and allowing him or her to test drive, not only are you building value in the vehicle, your guest also knows exactly what it is he or she is purchasing. The guest knows the vehicle inside and out. He or she has also driven the vehicle to know exactly how it drives. So once the guest verbally commits to buying the vehicle, then when you go to the negotiation process, your guest can't turn around and tell you that he or she still has not driven the vehicle or that he or she is unsure about any particular part of the vehicle because all of those objections should have been addressed during the presentation/demonstration process. If there are any objections or concerns about the specific vehicle, you need to overcome them prior to going to paper. These issues could be anything from fuel efficiency all the way to must-have safety features. Again, these are all things that should be discussed prior to landing your guest on a vehicle. The closer you get to landing a guest on a vehicle that has everything on his or her must-have list and wish list, the easier it will be for you to close that guest on the vehicle. You need to pay attention to the guest's hot buttons and work hard to find a vehicle that meets the guest's requirements. If you try and take shortcuts and find your guest a vehicle that doesn't have everything he or she is looking for, the chances of that guest being completely satisfied and buying the vehicle decrease. During your initial sit-down while you are filling out a guest sheet and finding out your guest's needs and wants, make sure you discuss trim levels and the extra costs that go with a higher trim level. That way you can clarify with your guest that he or she will have to pay a price according to the options he or she is requiring. Find out what kind of room your guest has in his or her budget to help you get the guest the best bang for his or her buck.

The final step before going to the negotiation process is getting verbal commitment from your guest on buying the vehicle. You want to make sure you have overcome every objection your guest may have had about the vehicle prior to closing the deal. By this time you should have already done a few different trial closes with your guest to make sure that he or she is on board. Here are a few trial closes for you to use when you are trying to wrap up a deal:

1.  I know you really loved the vehicle, guys! Before we go to a bill of sale, we need to go over the car proof and inspection, and then we'll wrap everything up.

2. Hey, guys, let's go grab the registration for your trade. My manager can't buy your car without it.

3. Which one of you will be registering the vehicle? I need to know which name to put on the bill of sale.

4. OK, guys, we drove three great vehicles. Which one did you guys want to go with?

5. That car drove sweet, man! Did you want me to order the aftermarket rims for it, or are you going to take it with the stock wheels?

6. It looks like we found the perfect car for you guys. Let's go have a seat at my desk. We need to work out some payment options for you before you sit down with my finance team.

7. Do you guys have an insurance company that you are currently dealing with, or did you need my help setting that up for you?

8. Hey, before we go over numbers, I'm just going to go tell my manager that you're super happy and that you have chosen to go with this vehicle.

9. Let's go enjoy a nice test drive. When we come back, we will see how close I can get you to your monthly budget. If you really love the car, I'll make sure my manager gets it done for you.

10. So, if I can make the numbers work and make this vehicle totally affordable and feasible within your budget, can we wrap this up right now?

Don't forget that these are just trial closes. You need to assume that your guest is buying. Using these lines will give you a good idea of where your guest's head is. A lot of times a guest is on board and follows your lead, but there are other times where your guest hesitates. Your confidence may come off as pushy to certain people. If you feel any hesitation from your guest, just continue with your process. Never push. You can always pull back and play it off as just a suggestion.

Get the commitment. Make sure your guest is completely satisfied with the vehicle before you go to paper. A lot of times customers will be unhappy about something and not tell you. Make sure you reiterate the fact that you've found the perfect vehicle and that your guest is completely satisfied with it. The harder you work on this step, the easier it will be to close a guest on monthly payments and get him or her into your finance office. Also, by taking the extra time to clarify that you've landed on the right vehicle, your guest won't second guess the deal when you are negotiating payments. You need to make sure the value of the vehicle outweighs the monthly payment.

### What Is Your Objection?

*"If you don't know what the objection is, how can you overcome it?"*

The golden rule to handling objections that your guest may have is being able to get him or her to tell you open and honestly what the objection is. It's easier said than done. A lot of times you may not be getting proper commitment from your guest even though you feel like everything is going smoothly. Don't be fooled. If your guest isn't committing to you and your product, there is a reason. Somewhere in your sales process you must have missed something.

As a salesperson in this industry, you need to understand that there will always be objections to handle with every guest. Sometimes the objections are big, and sometimes they are small. It's all about how you receive them. You need to be ready and waiting for an objection. The stronger you are, the more ammunition you have to help you handle every objection you receive. Once you can hear an objection and just handle it without getting nervous or hitting a roadblock, you're on your way to becoming a powerhouse objection handler.

> *Tip: To be the king of objection handling, you need to have a confident state of mind. Don't let an objection throw you off. You need to embrace objections with open arms. The more objections you handle, the stronger your car deal becomes. An objection is essentially another word for customer concern. If you identify and address these concerns, your guest stays informed and comfortable throughout the sale. Once you can master the art of objection handling, you will start to close deals that you once thought were going to be impossible.*

### Reflex Objections versus Real Objections

There are two types of objections. There are reflex objections, and there are also real objections or concerns. I'm going to help you identify the difference between these two. Not only that, I'm going to stock you up with loads of ammunition to help you overcome the most common objections in the business.

Reflex objections are basically things that your guests will respond to you by reflex based on the question you have asked. A lot of times when you hear these common objections, there is more truth behind them that you need to dig out. These objections can typically be overcome quite easily by a follow-up question. Here are some examples of reflex objections and how you can handle them:

*Customer Objection:*

"I need to do some research about the vehicle before I commit."

*Possible Responses:*

"Perfect! That's what I'm here for. What is it that you want to research? I'm sure I can help you find the answers you are looking for."

"Yeah, that's no problem at all! What information did you need me to provide you with in order for you to make a more educated decision?"

"That's totally understandable. Let's figure this out right now. What's your primary concern about this vehicle right at this moment?"

"OK, great! Is this vehicle missing something for you? If you're unsure about the vehicle, we can always go look at something else. What did you want to do research on?"

*Customer Objection:*

"This is the first place I stopped."

*Possible Responses:*

"Lucky me. I'm going to make sure this is the last place you stop. Whatever questions or concerns you have you can ask me. I'll be happy to be your car guy/gal."

"Great! Let's make this your last stop. I've found everything you wanted on your must-have list and more. Why would you want to go anywhere else?"

"So if I found you the perfect vehicle and got you everything you are looking for, there would be no reason for you to go anywhere else. I won't stop until you leave my dealership one hundred percent happy."

"We have over five hundred vehicles on the lot. I guarantee you that I will find you exactly what you are looking for. I'm going to help you find the perfect vehicle so you can get back to your everyday lifestyle…in style!"

*Customer Objection:*

"We just need to go home and think about it."

*Possible Responses:*

"No worries. What is it that you wanted to think about? Maybe I can help you out."

"OK, great! What's holding you guys back from making your decision right now? Is it the vehicle? Is it the price? Is it the payment? Is it the initial investment?"

"Earlier you told me if I found you the perfect vehicle I could earn your business. What are you guys unsure of? Let me know so I can make it work."

"Hey, look, we really need to wrap this up today. Let me know what it is that will make you guys happy enough right now to give me a high five and close the deal!"

"Guys, you are getting an amazing deal on this vehicle. It's a no-brainer. What do you need to think about?"

Those are a few examples of common objections. The main thing is that when you hear one of those objections you can't be afraid to ask why. You need to be strong enough to always have a rebuttal for whatever comes out of your guest's mouth. Dig deeper until you uncover the truth. Find out why your guest isn't happy or sure about the decision at hand. That way you have a better chance of overcoming the objection and getting a car deal.

Now, let's go over some real objections (concerns). These are real concerns your guest may have about your product or financing options. I'll go over a few and give you some more ammunition to help you overcome them.

*Customer Objection:*

"The dealership next door is offering me a better deal."

*Possible Responses:*

"You need to decide whether or not you would like to deal with me and my company. I hope I did a good enough job building value in our store and our product."

"We are giving you the best deal possible. They may have my price beat, but at the end of the day, what dealership do you feel will offer you the best customer service down the road? I guarantee you it will be from me."

"Are you comparing the exact same vehicle and trim level with the same kilometers?"

"Well, I can't offer you that same price; it's under market value. I can offer you nothing but the best customer service you could imagine long after you make your purchase with me."

*Customer Objection:*

"The interest rate is too high."

*Possible Responses:*

"I understand that you are paying a little bit of a higher interest rate. The interest rate you receive is a reflection of your credit. It is given to you by the banks, not us."

"The great thing is that the bank that's giving you the loan has a really great rebuilding program. In most cases, after one year of consistent payments, your application will be considered for review. At that point, we can look into getting you a better rate."

"You have to start somewhere. By taking on this loan, not only do you get a great vehicle, you are also on your way to getting your credit back on track."

"The loan you are taking on is open-ended, so you can pay it off as early as possible without any penalties or fees. If you do so, you don't have to pay the remaining interest when you buy out the vehicle because it is incurred monthly."

*Customer Objection:*

"I love the vehicle, but I'm just not ready to commit to making the payments."

*Possible Responses:*

"I know it's a big commitment for you, but at the end of the day, you're here because you need a vehicle. If you don't do this now, how are you going to get around?"

"The banks have already reviewed your income. They did their calculations, and based on your monthly income, this payment is within your budget. If they thought you couldn't afford the loan, they wouldn't give it to you."

"Hey, man, I know how much you love the car. Don't pass up this great deal; we already got this far. Let's just go for it. You only live once, and these are the things you need to enjoy!"

"You have a great opportunity here to take home a really sweet vehicle that I know you're going to love. Don't second guess yourself. I'm going to call one of my insurance brokers to see if I can save you some money on insurance."

Try out some of my closing lines next time you have the opportunity to do so. There is a line for every guest. Sit down with your coworkers and brainstorm some of your own. The more you have the better. Keep using the ones that you find most effective for you.

---

*Remember: The more you rehearse these lines, the more likely they will come out as second nature for you at the opportune time. This is a great way to always keep busy. One of the most effective ways to utilize your downtime is by training. It's what separates the good from the great.*

---

*Closing Trade-in Value*

Working a deal with a trade is always tricky. It's just one more obstacle you have to overcome. A lot of times people will trust in you and your dealership to do a proper evaluation on their trade. Other times people will come in expecting to get full retail value for their trade and whole-sale pricing on the vehicle they are trying to buy. I've lost many deals due to issues with trade-in value. Sometimes it's just inevitable that you and your guest cannot agree on numbers. I'll go over the most effective ways to handle trade-in value so that you can use them the next time you find yourself working a car deal with a trade involved.

Right off the bat, you will find out if your guest is planning to trade in a vehicle. It's probably one of the most important qualifying questions for you to ask. By finding out the specifications of the vehicle (year, kilometers, trim level), you should have a good idea of the vehicle's wholesale value. If you don't, I'm sure your manager will. Your guest may want to know what his or her trade is worth well before looking at any of your vehicles. That means they are purely shopping to get the best trade-in value. Don't play that hand right away. By giving your guest a number, he or she now knows what your dealership is offering, and your guest will then get up and go to the next dealership and ask them to beat your offer. The most effective way to overcome this objection without turning your guest off and not answering his or her question (giving them a big no) is to give them an in and around number ranging from high to low.

*Guest*: "I'd like to know what my trade is worth before we look at any vehicles."

*Salesperson*: "No, worries. Here at our dealership we actually have to do a full vehicle appraisal to give you an accurate trade-in value. I'd be happy to give you an average wholesale number of what a vehicle like yours is selling for."

*Guest*: "OK."

*Salesperson*: A vehicle like yours, depending on its condition, will range from eight thousand dollars all the way to fourteen thousand dollars Let's go outside and find a vehicle you are happy to own. Once we do, we will do a full vehicle appraisal on your trade and get you as much money back as possible for it."

By giving your guest a number that ranges from low to high, you don't have to commit to a number right from the get-go. Also, it gives you a chance to default back to your sales process. You answered your guest's question. Even though you never gave them a clear-cut answer, your guest should now understand that it makes sense for you to say that you need to do a full vehicle appraisal to give them an accurate number. How can you give your guest a trade-in value before you or your manager ever look at his or her car?

Actual trade-in value should never be discussed until the negotiation process; by this time, you would already have landed your guest on a new vehicle that he or she is excited to purchase. You have gone through your trial closes and have gotten verbal commitment from your guest to purchase your vehicle as long as the numbers work. The reason I don't like to get into the trade-in value until the end is because I don't want the trade to be in the spotlight.

As a salesperson, you want to keep your focus on the new vehicle. Keep reminding your guest that he or she is about to drive away in a vehicle that has everything your guest wants and more. Your goal is to get your guest so excited about the new vehicle that the trade-in value all of a sudden becomes less important. So if a guest came in expecting to get

$10,000, but after a full vehicle appraisal left getting $8,000, it doesn't matter anyway, because in the end, the guest left with exactly what he or she wanted—the vehicle of his or her dreams!

*Guest*: "My trade is worth more. I want more money for it."

This is where you have an opportunity to make or break your car deal. I'm going to help you paint the perfect picture in your guest's mind of what it takes to sell a car privately and why it's just easier to meet you somewhere in between and sell it to you.

*Salesperson*: "Well, guys, after our appraisal, the actual trade-in value for your vehicle is seven thousand dollars."

*Guest*: "My trade is worth more. I want eleven thousand dollars for it."

*Salesperson*: "I understand. What are you basing your numbers on?"

*Guest*: "I've been checking to see what people are asking for the same or similar vehicle on Kijiji and Autotrader, and I think eleven thousand dollars is a fair number."

*Salesperson*: "OK, let me ask you a question. If you were to post your vehicle on Kijiji for eleven thousand dollars, you would have to take calls and book appointments for people to come view your vehicle. After they test drive it, they will more than likely want to take it for an independent inspection. During that time, you will be without a vehicle. During their inspection, they will come back to you with at least a couple of thousand dollars in reconditioning costs (these are reconditioning costs that you have already accounted for during your appraisal) and ask you to discount it to eight thousand or nine thousand dollars. After going through that a few times, you'd eventually end up selling it for that price, right? Why don't I save you all

that time and heartache and talk to my manager about stepping up
to seventy-five hundred dollars or maybe even eight thousand dollars just so we can wrap this up right now?"

By explaining to your guest the daunting task of selling a car privately
and allowing him or her to visualize, step by step, the horror that he or
she will have to go through, when you ask your guest to lighten up and
meet you at an agreeable number, he or she will be more willing to say
OK. By this point, if you sell what you're saying hard enough, your guest
will think that you are doing him or her a favor by taking the trade off
his or her hands. This is a close that needs to be rehearsed. Practice it
until this close is implanted in your brain, and the next time you get the
opportunity to use it, just go for it. You're going to be amazed by how
often it works!

### Trade Appraisals

Most dealerships, if not all, have trade appraisal forms that will help
you accurately appraise a vehicle by asking the right questions about it.
The final trade-in value will more than likely be determined by your
manager after he or she goes to evaluate and drive the trade-in vehicle.
Depending on how good you are at filling out a trade appraisal, your
manager may not even have to do much in this process.

A good trade appraisal will have questions on it that are set up in a way
that will give you an opportunity to devalue your customer's trade.

How do you devalue a customer trade-in vehicle? Well, it's actually pretty
simple. To properly devalue a customer trade, your primary focus needs
to be on maintenance and reconditioning costs.

Your first step is to walk around the trade-in vehicle with your guest and
point out any body damage (dents and scratches) you may see. Make

sure when you point any damage out that don't mention anything verbally. Just simply touch every imperfection you notice with your hands. Your guest will also make mental notes of all the imperfections you've discovered. Touch the tires, and check the tread life left. If the windshield is cracked, touch it and make a note on your appraisal. Every time you find an imperfection and point it out, your guest is mentally devaluing his or her own vehicle. The more imperfections you discover, the easier it is for you to turn around and explain to your guest why he or she is getting a number less than what he or she initially expected upon arrive at your dealership.

Next, you want to ask your guest questions about his or her current maintenance cycle. Find out for how long the guest has owned the vehicle. How many kilometers does he or she put on per year? Is it more than the average amount? How often does the guest have oil changes? How often does he or she service the transmission? Have the guest ever changed the brakes? Does the guest follow factory-recommended maintenance? The more of these questions you ask, and the more nos you hear, the better. What you're doing is exposing the fact that the vehicle you just appraised is going to have a reconditioning cost added to it in order to be able to retail it again. If you bring that to the surface, your guest will be less likely to turn down your trade-in offer.

Try some of these tips the next time you go out to appraise a vehicle. Don't take any shortcuts. You need to take your time while doing a trade appraisal. Don't look at it as just another step you need to complete before you can get to a bill of sale. Take it seriously, and use this opportunity to devalue every trade-in. The extra five to ten minutes it takes to do a proper trade appraisal will pay off in the long run, and you will close more people on trade-in value by doing it the right way than if you don't.

As a salesman, I have learned something. I have learned that in this industry you are going to come across a whole lot of people with a whole lot of objections. Some are going to be real, and the others are just lies. Some people will say anything just to get out of your grasp. I have come to the realization that there is no salesperson in the world who can close everyone. Not me, not you, and also not the best of the best, most renowned sales gurus. This doesn't mean that you are not great at what you do; it means that there is a perfect time for everyone to buy a car. There will always be someone who can find a better deal down the road. There will always be someone who gets cold feet and stops answering your calls because that person doesn't want to take on the payments. There will always the person who ends up buying a car privately. There will always be that person who just didn't like your style even though you thought you were on your A game while dealing with him or her. It happens to me, and it will happen to you. Realize it and toughen up. For every guest who walks out on you and stops replying to your phone calls, text messages, and e-mails, get out there and find five more! It's part of the game. All you can do is get in front of every opportunity that is presented to you and do what you do best.

# Chapter 3:
# The Almighty Follow-up

*"If you're going to call me to get my attention,
make sure you have a good reason to call."*

Let's get right into every salesperson's favorite part of the job: following up with guests who more than likely don't want to be followed up with. If anyone read that first line and agreed with me, shame on you. Following up is not a chore. It's a responsibility! It's part of the job. You need to grasp that fact and embrace it. Following up is the last step in my "Seven Steps of Selling" that I shared with you in Chapter 2.

Customers like to be followed up with; they just don't like to be bothered and harassed by salespeople if those people have nothing to offer them. Following up with your guests is done for numerous reasons, whether you're trying to get them into your dealership to try out some vehicles and make a purchase or whether you're just following up to see how a guest's New Year's party was. There are many great reasons to follow up with your guests, and I'm going to go over these different areas of follow-up so that you can tap into a great source of business that sometimes goes uncharted by many salespeople. By following up with your guests properly, you should be able to double your volume in no time.

## Dealing with Rejection

Getting rejected in this business is inevitable. It's going to happen to you over and over again. Don't you worry, because just like it's happening to you, it's happening to every other salesperson across the globe. There's nothing you can do to change the fact that some people just don't want to buy from you, or they got a better deal down the road, or they came into your dealership impulsively with no intentions of ever buying a car. These things happen, so don't be so hard on yourself. You don't suck! What you do need to understand is that rejection is inevitable, so don't get discouraged when it happens to you. Statistics say that you should roughly be closing one out of every four opportunities that you are given. That's only 25 percent, and if you're doing that, you are considered a rock star! With that in mind, imagine how many times, over and over again, the greatest and strongest salespeople in the world have been rejected.

When you get rejected, this is just another opportunity to understand why the particular guest is rejecting you. Is it you? Did you rub the guest the wrong way? Is it your product? Is it your price? Is it just not the opportune time for the guest to buy? Were all of the decision makers present? Did you miss a step in the sales process? Or maybe you just couldn't come to terms and agree on a deal that was a win-win for the both of you. The reason doesn't matter as long as you learn from it and move forward.

You need to brush off every rejection as if it never happened. It's always on to the next opportunity. Keep talking to every opportunity you can; the more people you get in front of or talk to on the phone, the higher the odds are of you hearing yes. Just be prepared to filter out all of the guests who are going to tell you no. If there is one tip I could give to all the salespeople in the world it would be to **never** take anything a customer says personally, and **always** take your attitude and energy and focus it on your next deal.

You need to be able to identify real opportunities to sell a car when they are presented to you, as opposed to time-wasting opportunities. People who remain actively in contact with you are serious buyers who are willing to spend their money with you; they just have not seen or been presented with something that possesses enough value for them, or they have not found anything that meets all of their requirements.

How many times have you made a follow-up call and the guest on the other line sounded less than impressed to hear from you? It happens a lot. You are calling these guests as a salesperson who's always trying to sell them something. It doesn't have to be like that. We are living in the twenty-first century, and we need to step up our game. Our old sales tactics are getting dry from being overly exposed. We need new tactics. We need to take a different approach. Let's go over a standard follow-up call and compare it with some new, fresh, and innovative ways to follow up.

### Standard Follow-up Call

Salesperson: "Good morning, Mr. Johnson. This is Derek calling from Go Auto. How you doing today?"

Customer: "I'm doing fine. How can I help you?"

Salesperson: "I was just calling to see if you had a chance to talk to your wife about that new Ford F150 you test drove yesterday?"

Customer: "Yes, I talked it over with my wife. We're still not completely sold. We might just keep looking. She says she would prefer an SUV. I'm still pushing for a truck."

Salesperson: "OK, great. Is there anything else I can do to help you guys make a decision? Maybe you guys should both come down, and I can show you guys some SUV options."

Customer: "I'll talk to the wife and get back to you."

Salesperson: "Sounds great. Thanks for your time, sir."

That is your typical, average follow-up call made by your typical, average salesperson. There was no excitement, no determination, and most importantly there was nothing offered by the salesperson to entice the customer into ever walking back into the store again. Let's try to go about the follow-up call a different way.

*Salesperson*: "Good morning, Mr. Johnson. This is Derek calling from Go Auto. How are you doing today?"

*Customer*: "I'm doing just fine, thanks. How can I help you?"

*Salesperson*: "I hope you're sitting down. I have some cool information about that that F150 you test drove yesterday. I just found out that that specific model comes in Ruby Red and Sunset Red. I know you were debating whether or not you would like a darker red tone, and I have two available for you!"

*Customer*: "Oh, really? They weren't there yesterday?"

*Salesperson*: "They just landed this morning. When I saw the trucks pull up, I thought of you and jumped out of my chair. You should be receiving an e-mail any minute. I sent you a quick thirty-second walk-around video of both trucks. Watch both videos and let me know what color you would prefer. Just call me back when you get the e-mail."

*Customer*: "Well, all right. I'll take a look at them and call you back."

*Salesperson*: "That's perfect! When should I expect your call?"

*Customer*: "Just give me five minutes."

*Salesperson*: "Sounds good. I'll talk to you shortly."

So in this follow-up call I accomplished two things. Instead of asking the guest if he is ever coming back, I took initiative and gave he and his wife a good reason to come back by going out of my way to send a quick thirty-second video of a similar truck of interest in a preferred color. This shows the guest that I take my job seriously and that I am prepared to go the extra mile to earn his business. Another thing I did was that I built a form of trust with my guest by telling him to review the new information I sent him and requesting for him to call me back, throwing the ball in his court for a quick period in order to make him feel like he's in control of the sale. Now when he calls back, I need to handle any objections he has and get him back through the door.

*Salesperson*: "Thanks for holding. This is Derek, and who am I speaking with, please?"

*Customer*: "Hey, Derek, it's Mr. Johnson returning your call. I just checked out those videos, and let me tell you, I would definitely go with the Ruby Red. But my wife isn't completely sold on a truck. She's still pushing for an SUV."

*Salesperson*: "No worries, Mr. Johnson. Has your wife had a chance to check out the trucks as well?"

*Customer*: "No, not yet."

*Salesperson*: "I have an idea. Why don't you and your wife come in tonight so I can show you guys this truck in person, and at the same time I will go over some SUV options with you guys, and from there we will make a decision and determine what would be the most feasible option for you and your family."

*Customer*: "OK, Derek, that sounds great. Let me talk to my wife and get back to you."

*Salesperson*: "Yes, for sure. Let me check my schedule real quick. I'm available at five forty-five p.m. or seven fifteen p.m. Which one of those times do you think would be best for you guys to come in?"

*Customer*: "Probably five forty-five p.m."

*Salesperson*: "OK, I'm just going to schedule you in for five forty-five p.m. You talk to your wife, and I'll see you in a few hours. If anything changes, just let me know."

*Customer*: "OK, we shall see you tonight."

*Salesperson*: "Take care now, Mr. Johnson."

I have accomplished a great deal at this moment. I've revamped my guest's excitement about my product and handled his objections. I also rebooked him with all of the decision makers to come down to finalize a purchase. That's just one way to make an effective follow-up call. Let's go over other strategies you can use when making follow-up calls.

*By the Way...*

Try using the "by the way" strategy. When you're calling a guest, just call to see how his or her day is going. Start up a conversation with the guest, or maybe call the guest with some source of new information that's relevant to his or her purchase. Then, when the opportunity presents itself, say, "By the way, did you get a chance to review my e-mail?" or "By the way, did you end up getting those paystubs sorted out for me?" or "By the way, how's that insurance coming along? Did you need my help setting it up?"

This strategy works best when you already have an established relationship with your guest. Spark up a conversation with your guest first, even though you have an ulterior motive to gather a piece of information that you need. This strategy will make the ulterior motive appear to be like an afterthought, even though it is the sole purpose of your call. It's a simple strategy that's purpose is for you to come across as a friend as opposed to just another businessperson trying to close a deal.

*Business Development Center*

Try taking a different approach. With this strategy you will need another salesperson on board. Swap a list of prospects that you couldn't close for whatever reason but that you feel that there is still life in the deal. These should be guests who you know are buyers, but you feel like you've exhausted all your tools and you really have no other angle to take with them. Swap lists and call every guest with this approach:

> *Salesperson*: "Hi, my name is Derek, and I'm calling from Go Auto's business development center. I know you recently visited one of our stores. I was just calling hoping to get some quick feedback from you and find out how your experience was while you were in our store."

By using that as your opening line, you are not identifying yourself as a salesperson. You are identifying yourself as a Go Auto employee who was put in place to call previous guests to get feedback on guest experiences. The great thing about this opening line is that guests are one hundred times more likely to open up to someone from a business development center as opposed to an actual salesperson because they don't suspect or feel like that person is trying to sell them anything. What they don't know is that you know exactly what happened when they were at the dealership. What you're doing is waiting for them to explain to you what happened when they were in the store. Be prepared to hear complaints and long stories. Once they are done explaining to you what happened and why they never ended up making a purchase, find a moment to ask them this question:

*Salesperson*: "Oh, really? So I take it you already bought a vehicle somewhere else?"

If they say yes, then you thank them for their time and let them know that you and your company would be happy to get another opportunity to earn their business.

If they say no to the question, then you want to slowly take the conversation in this direction:

*Salesperson*: "Oh. You never purchased a vehicle yet? I'll tell you what I'm going to do. I'm about to forward an e-mail to the general manager of the dealership, and I'll send him all the details of what your experience was like. What the GM will do is review the information and look for a way to turn around your experience completely and make you happy. It usually takes about fifteen minutes for me to get a response. Once I do, though, I'll call you back to let you know what the GM has sorted out for you. How does that sound?"

*Customer*: "That sounds fair. I'll be waiting for your call."

*Salesperson*: "Perfect, I'll talk to you soon."

If you get this far, you are one step away from booking an appointment. Informing the guest that you are going to get the general manager involved and going the extra mile to earn the guest's business gives the guest a feeling of self-worth. Your goal is to make the guest feel so great and so important that he or she is happy to come back into to the dealership to see what you guys have to offer. The second call is when you're going to go for an appointment. It should go something like this:

*Salesperson*: "Hello, Mr. Perry. It's Derek calling you back from Go Auto. I got some great news. I just got off the phone with the general manager of the store, and he's very upset that you felt like your experience in his store was anything less than perfect. He actually asked me if I would meet you at the dealership and personally take care of you and help you out through your entire vehicle purchase. He also wants to know when our appointment is so he can make it a point to be there. He will be involved throughout the whole process, and this time around we are going to collectively make sure you leave our dealership one hundred percent satisfied. What is your schedule looking like tomorrow?"

And just like that, you have locked down a new appointment and a new opportunity to get a car deal. This is a unique approach to take. Your general manager obviously needs to be on board because his or her involvement is key to making these types of deals happen. Call it a VIP appointment because, throughout the whole sale, you need to play the role as if you are literally at the dealership for the sole purpose of making sure that the particular guest gets the best customer service in history. If you can master this strategy, you will officially be on another level of sales that most salespeople never get to. Give it a shot and see and feel for yourself what kind of energy you can create during these sales. You'll be amazed.

*Sorry, I Stepped Out...*

Use this strategy when you have to follow up with a guest who didn't show up for his or her appointment. If you're calling a guest who didn't show up for his or her appointment, a good way to call the guest without having to call him or her out for not showing up for the appointment is to flip the script completely. Call the guest and tell him or her this:

*Salesperson*: "Hey, George, it's Derek calling from Go Auto. I just called to apologize. I had to step out of the dealership to deliver a vehicle to one of my guests. I just got back. My receptionist told me I had some guests waiting for me. I hope you guys didn't wait too long. Are you still close by?"

Your guest will answer one of two ways. Most of the time, he or she will be honest with you and tell you that it wasn't him or her who was at the store and that he or she also got tied up and couldn't make the appointment. At that time you can joke it off as no big deal and reschedule the guest for later that day or the following day. It's always good to do a little more investigating into why the guest never made the appointment, because if the guest missed the first appointment, he or she may have a reason why the appointment was missed that he or she just isn't telling you.

There will be other times when the guest will just follow your lead and tell you that yes, in fact, he or she was at the dealership waiting for you. At that point you need to just go along with the guest and apologize once more and reschedule him or her for as soon as possible.

The reason this strategy is effective is because you're taking away all the guilt the guest may have from standing you up. A lot of times when a guest no-shows his or her appointment and you're constantly trying to reschedule him or her, the guest may feel too embarrassed to even step foot into your dealership. Also, if a guest continues to not show up for his or her appointment and you continue to call the guest and tell him or her that it's OK and you keep trying to reschedule him or her, this shows the guest that you're desperate for a deal and that your time is not valuable to you; it just sets a bad tone for the sale if the guest ever does show up, because he or she will just continue to try and dictate the sale while there at the dealership. If you're not in control of your sale from step one, you will never be able to control the outcome. A huge part of being successful in closing deals is having the ability to stay in control of your guests in an elusive sort of way where they don't know what you're doing or where you're going with the sale. They are just along for the ride. However, you know the whole time what you're doing and what the next steps are for you to take.

*Great News, Guys...*

Calling anyone with great news is always a great idea. It doesn't matter if it's a business call or a personal call. Great news is exactly what it sounds like. It's great news! It doesn't matter what the news is as long as you are excited enough to sell it. Everybody loves to hear great news. Don't you? When was the last time someone called you and said, "Hey, I have some great news for you"? It's been a while, right?

When you call a guest, the great news can be that you found a particular vehicle that your guest was interested in, or the great news can be that it's twenty-plus degrees outside. Regardless of what the great news is, it's your excitement and charisma that's going to sell it. Have an underlying purpose for making the call, but start it off with a very energetic "Hey, I have great news for you!" This is where you need to sell off of emotion to get people through the door.

*Surprise for You...*

Have some fun with your guests. Follow-up calls don't have to be boring. Who doesn't love a good surprise? I know I do. So why not pique your guest's interest with a phone call letting him or her know that you have a surprise waiting for him or her the next time he or she comes down to the store. The surprise can be anything from a preferred vehicle that the guest mentioned he or she would like to test drive to a simple five-dollar gift card to the guest's favorite coffee shop. Just make sure not to spill the surprise until the guest comes down to the dealership. The goal is to hype the surprise up so well that the guest's desire to know what the surprise is will drive him or her to your store faster and get him or her more excited to get there. It sets a good tone for your sale.

Try out these strategies when you're making your follow-up calls. At the same time, sit down with a group of salespeople and brainstorm your own follow-up strategies to use in your day-to-day operations. Remember that not every strategy works on every guest. I'll leave it up to you to determine which strategies work best with each individual guest. Base your strategy selection on the strength of the relationship you have formed with the guest.

*Phone Tip: The Phantom Text*

Do you have a guest who you feel is avoiding your calls? Someone who you are following up with but you feel like you are wasting your time, but you don't want to kill the lead? Try this. Grab a friend or coworker's cell phone and text your guest. The text should look exactly like this:

"Hey, Jimmy. Call me."

Watch what happens within seconds. You will get a response that looks like this:

"Who's this?"

The minute you get that response, you know, first of all, that your guest is still alive and well, and then you can confirm that, yes, indeed, your calls and texts are being avoided. Once the guest answers the text, send a follow-up text stating your name and the company you work for. At this point the guest will either tell you that he or she is not interested anymore, or the guest just won't respond to your text again. This is a great way to get closure to a lead. Once you have gotten closure, you can then move on to the next opportunity.

## Repeats and Referrals

This is an area that we as salespeople are all familiar with, yet much of the time it's a part of our business that goes untapped. We all hear the term repeat *and referral business,* but how many of us really understand the concept and the benefits of focusing our time and energy in this sector.

Focusing on repeat business as well as getting referrals from previously sold guests is one of the best things you can do to elevate your game on the sales floor. The question is, what's the most effective way to do this? There are salespeople who have been in the business so long that they don't even take walk-in traffic or sales calls because they are too busy dealing with repeat and referral business. That is a great spot to be in. If you ask any one of them if they would trade that for all the ups and the sales calls in the world, I guarantee you they would say no. If you have gotten the opportunity to deal with repeat guests and guests who get referred to you from previous guests who have promoted your services, you know that it's a hell of a lot easier to capitalize on these opportunities. If you are dealing with a guest who you have sold a vehicle to in the past, that person obviously came back to you because he or she liked you and the customer service you provided him or her with. So when you go to sell them the second time around, it's an easy-breezy sale because you guys already have an established relationship.

It's more or less the same concept for referral business. A referral is a guest who seeks you out because he or she has heard from a friend or family member that you have provided great customer service in the past. These are guests who have found their way to you through word of mouth. If you have your previous guests promoting your services to their friends and family, then when the guest who has been referred actually comes in to deal with you, there is already a level of trust established because you guys are bonded through your mutual friend. Now, when you go to close up the deal, the odds are that your guest will trust you enough to say yes!

So if you know that the odds of selling repeat and referral guests are heavily in your favor, why aren't you focusing on these guests as much as you are focusing on your sales leads and walk-in traffic leads? I'll tell you why. It's because it takes more work. That reminds me of a saying I heard in a sales book I read called *The Sales Bible* by Jeffrey Gitomer. He said, "Most people aren't willing to do the hard work it takes to making selling easy." When I read that quote, it stuck in my brain. I thought about how true it was. Selling is easy, but in order to make it easy, you need to understand the process and implement little systems within your own day-to-day operations that set you up to create more opportunities, and inevitably sell more cars. The systems are all available to you; it's just a matter of implementing and capitalizing on them.

> *Tip: If you really want to grow in this business, the amount of time you spend learning and training yourself to understand the basic principles of sales will play a big factor in how far you go. The second you believe that you have learned everything about the industry and that there is nothing more you could possibly know is the second you will stop growing.*

You need a system that will help you track and command repeat and referral business. The extra work you do putting a system in place that will effectively help you utilize your clientele base so that your repeat and referral business can grow will be the deciding factor in whether or not you can make this area in your business grow beyond your wildest dreams. If you're willing to put in the work, I'm willing to give you an effective system you can put in place to get you started.

## *Repeat Business*

Let's start by tracking your sold customers. If you're going to success-fully be able to capitalize on repeat business, you need to successfully be able to track your sold guests. You should be looking to all your sold guests to potentially make a purchase from you every year or so. It will be a different scenario for every guest. If you are selling new cars, you are going to want to follow up with your sold guests every year to present all of your latest and greatest new products. The great thing about selling new cars is that manufacturers are continuing to engineer upgraded models with new features that are designed to excite buyers and take the manufacturer's product to the next level. Talking about new models is a great way to get your previous guests through the door.

The same concept applies for used vehicles. A lot of times when you are selling used vehicles, you may be selling these vehicles at higher interest rates. Also, because of such a wide span of financing rates and terms on used vehicles, used buyers sometimes compromise with what they really want to buy in order to maintain a comfortable monthly payment. There is always a reason to get your previous guests through the door, whether it's to upgrade their car or put them in a better financial situation by lowering their interest rates.

Most of the dealerships out there have computer systems that help you track all of your guests. A lot of these systems work well. It's never a bad idea to have a paper system in place as well to help you track your progress. Here's my deal tracker system. I'll go over every column and explain its importance too.

| DATE | NAME | PHONE/E-MAIL | VEHICLE SOLD | LENDER | APR? |
|------|------|--------------|--------------|--------|------|
|      |      |              |              |        |      |
|      |      |              |              |        |      |
|      |      |              |              |        |      |
|      |      |              |              |        |      |

*Date*

You always put the date that you sold the guest so that when you come back to the tracker months down the road you know exactly when your guest purchased from you. This will help you stay organized and aware of exactly when you last dealt with every guest. This will also come in handy when you are making your refinancing calls.

*Name*

Always put the first and last lame of the sold guest. It's also a good idea to put the guest's spouse's name, if applicable, and the names of their children. Remembering someone's spouse's name and children's names a year down the road will earn you some major points with your guest.

*Contact Info*

Write down any and every phone number you have for every guest, along with e-mail addresses. A lot of people change their numbers frequently. It's always good to get into the habit of getting alternate phone numbers and e-mail addresses. The more contact information you can get, the better. This will make it easier for you to get in touch with all your guests a year or two down the road.

*Vehicle Sold*

Write down the year, make, model, and kilometers of the vehicle you sold. The more information you log about the vehicle your guest bought, the better it will serve you as a reference when you call the guest down the road to upgrade the vehicle. Don't forget things like color and trim level. Those kinds of things might come in handy.

*Lending Institution*

Keep a record of what lending institution is financing each of your guests. Again, it's a good reference for you. Also, when you go to make contact with your guest a year from now, you will look very professional when you have all of the guest's information memorized. It will also work to your advantage if you know of any new incentives a certain bank is offering. This gives you an opportunity to call all your guests who are currently financing with a particular bank and get them into your dealership to take advantage of the new incentives.

*APR (Approved Interest Rate)*

Write down what interest rates your guests are signing up for. This is especially useful for your subprime guests. The majority of subprime lenders lend at a higher interest rate, but in return, they have really good refinancing programs. In most cases, after ten to twelve months of successful payment history, subprime lenders will consider lowering their interest rates on the next loan. That is a great, if not the greatest, reason to give a previous guest a call back a year later. If you take the financial approach, there are not too many people who would not have an open ear to you if you can lower their interest rate.

Now that you have a deal tracker to go by, there should be no reason for you not to capitalize on repeat business. This chart will help you manage your repeat business properly and professionally. Let's just say you are selling ten cars a month. Now, every month you have another ten opportunities to capitalize on your previous guests. If you close 50 percent of those opportunities, you have just increased your volume by 50 percent. With this system alone, you can go from selling, on average, ten cars a month all the way up to fifteen. If you start today, you will reap the rewards ten months down the road.

When you make these calls to your previous guests, have some sort of strategy for every call. Again, here we are in the twenty-first century where our old sales tactics just don't cut it anymore. These calls are super important, because if you make them properly, you will have a very high closing ratio on them. Consider them just as important as the Glengarry Glenn Ross leads from the 1992 film *Glengarry Glen Ross* (an old-school sales movie definitely worth the hour and a half of your time).

I'm going to go over a few different scenarios you will come across and give you a few good pitches to use when you are looking to make contact with your previously sold guests.

*New Model*

This is one of the most common scenarios you will run into selling new cars—trying to get your previous guest to come in and check out the latest and greatest models your manufacturer has to offer. Take advantage of the Internet. Prepare a quick two-minute video of the new models you are trying to promote alongside a little rundown of the vehicles' new features and benefits. Send the e-mail out to all of the previously sold guests you are targeting. Once you send out the e-mail, start making some calls. Use your newly acquired strategy to get your guests excited, and make sure they get their eyes on the video. It's one thing to talk up your new products, but it's another to let your guests visualize them on short video.

*"The bank e-mailed my store..."*

This is a great line to use when you are trying to get your previous guests through the door to refinance a new vehicle. It's most effective on those guests who have signed with you previously at a higher interest rate. When you make these calls, take the financial approach. Go through you're deal tracker and call all your guests who signed on at a higher interest rate ten months ago or more. Tell them that you have great news and that the lending institution they signed with e-mailed your finance team to inform them that they are ready to review applications for lower interest rates on a new car. This pitch is meant to focus on getting the guests' interest rate down so that they can pay down their principle faster. The bonus is that guests get to upgrade their vehicle at the same time. You need to put in the work to get them a lower interest rate, and in return, you will benefit by getting another car deal. It's a win-win situation for all.

*"How are you enjoying your vehicle?"*

This is a follow-up call you should be making with each and every one of your sold guests every three to six months. When you make these calls, it's important not to try and sell anything. The sole purpose of these calls is to genuinely find out how your guests are enjoying their vehicles. At the same time, it's an opportunity for you to make contact with them and let them know that you're still around and that you still care. It creates a solid foundation for your relationships down the road. Find out how the car is working for them, and try to get a little personal too. Ask them how their careers are going and wish them the best. Also, let them know that you will be touching base with them in another few months to make sure that they are still 100 percent satisfied. Even though you may think that these calls are ineffective because you don't get the deal now, these calls will pay off in the long run because your guests will never forget about you the next time they are in the market for a new vehicle. Not only that, the next time one of your guests is with a friend or family member who mentions that he or she is in the market for a vehicle, your previous guests will be sure to promote you in a positive way because of your exceptional customer service. This will bring you more referral business than you ever thought possible. This is nothing new in sales, yet it's a strategy that often goes untapped because a lot of salespeople can only focus on getting the prize right now, which is great, but they fail to see the reward that will come by putting themselves out there and making sure their services aren't forgotten by their clientele base. If you ever find yourself with some downtime, these calls are what you should be focusing on.

Now, let's say you're making these calls and you make contact with one of your guests. The guest explains to you that he or she isn't happy with his or her vehicle. Maybe it just doesn't have enough room for the family, or maybe it was an impulse purchase and after some consideration, it hasn't turned out to be feasible for the guest at this point in his or her life. Maybe the guest bought a used vehicle that didn't turn out to be mechanically sound. Whatever the reason, by making the call, you have just created an opportunity to get the guest back into you're dealership to consider trading in for a new vehicle that is more suitable to his or her current needs. These calls are a win-win situation for you. Nothing bad can come from them. They only create opportunity for you in different ways. By putting this strategy in full effect, you will never *not* have anything to do again!

Try out the strategies I have given to you, and see how effectively they work for you. The key to being successful in the sales industry is being able to put in the hard work that the next person isn't willing to put in. When it comes to repeat business, the above strategies are the ones that I have found to be most effective. However, it's never a bad idea to have a brainstorming session with a group of salespeople to see what other strategies get brought to the table. My question is, how serious are you about becoming the best? You need to create your own opportunities and not wait for the opportunities to come to you. Don't leave the fate of your success to chance. To be a great salesperson, these are the things you have to do in order to achieve new levels of success.

## *Referral Business*

How great a feeling is it to be sitting at your desk with no scheduled appointments, only to have your receptionist page you to the front desk and inform you that you have a guest waiting? You have a guest at reception who you have never met nor spoken to who has just requested to deal with you specifically. Awesome, right? It's called a referral. Someone out there—more than likely one of your previous guests—has enjoyed you and your customer service enough to promote your name and refer you to one of his or her friends or family members.

Now think about how often that happens to you. Has it happened one time? Can you count how many times it's happened to you on one hand? Does it happen to you so often that it's just regular business for you? If you answered yes to any other question but the last one, good job, but you still have some work to do.

Just like repeat business, referral business is just as important for you to capitalize on if you want to hit the same numbers as all of the big hitters out there. Repeats and referrals go hand in hand. You're going to have your clientele base, and from them you need to not only try to make them repeat guests, you also want to get referral business from them as well. The most obvious way to do that is through great customer service, but that's a given. What you need to do is put a system in place that will insure you referral business by getting commitment from your sold guests to send you referrals.

If you can get every one of your sold guests to send you one referral per month, imagine how many more opportunities you can create to sell more cars and generate more repeat business. Your clientele base will grow, along with the names on your deal tracker. You will have more business than ever coming from these two networking systems. Add them to all the sales calls, walk-ins, and any other sources of leads your dealership may offer and your portfolio will consistently expand, and you will find yourself getting busier and busier.

A lot of dealerships and major corporations out there understand the importance of referrals, enough so that they have referral systems in place that offer up to $500 per referral. That's a pretty sweet incentive just for promoting a certain store or group. But as an individual sales-person looking to expand his or her clientele base, you don't have to stop there. Why not go above and beyond and create your own referral system?

*Network Your Own Referral System*

> *Tip: In order to get a referral, you need to earn one! If one of your guests is going to refer someone to you, then they need to trust you enough and feel comfortable enough with you to put their loved ones in your hands. They need to know that you will take care of them as if they are family.*

From the time you start your sale to the time you wrap up your sale and you're prepared to deliver a vehicle to your guest, you and your guest should have a solid relationship established. Get into the habit of getting your guests to commit to sending you one referral a month. Throwing in a little incentive will always help. It can be anything from one hundred dollars cash all the way to a couple of oil changes on the house, above and beyond any dealer incentive. These incentives will go a long way. Don't be afraid to get creative and think outside the box when you are giving individual guests incentives to drive business your way. Offer each guest an incentive that you believe will trigger him or her to actively promote your services and send business your way. The greater the reward, the higher the odds are of your guests to actually go out of their way to send you business.

*Favor for a Favor*

Depending on what type of business or occupation your guest is in, you will come across opportunities to start a two-way referral program. For every referral one of your guests sends you, you do some networking for your guest and get him or her one referral right back. For example, if you sell a vehicle to a guest who is an insurance broker, refer one of your guests to him or her, and in return he or she will refer a guest right back to you. Now you have just created a mutual business relationship. It's a big win-win situation for the both of you.

Let's say you can create one solid business relationship per month, and every relationship is sending you one referral per month. After one year, you would have twelve solid relationships sending you one solid referral per month. That is a total of 144 referrals sent your way in just one year. If you're closing an average of 80 percent of your referrals, you would close an extra 115 deals per year! You can potentially close more deals a year than an average salesperson just off of a simple referral program. Keep in mind that this is above and beyond all of your regular business sales. Now that I put it in perspective for you, doesn't it make sense to take some time and strategize on how you can get this plan into motion? Start by prospecting good candidates to promote this program. The sooner you find twelve guests who are on board, the faster you can get referrals flooding your phone asking for you to earn their business. Just remember to find candidates who you know you will be able to send referrals back to.

As you can see, there are many great ways to follow up. Follow up with all of your guests as often as possible. Start implementing some of your newly acquired strategies and see which ones work best for you. Don't be afraid to think outside of the box. Create your own strategies as well so that you always have fresh pitches to use. Following up should always be fun and exciting for you and for your guests.

One of the main things for you to take from this chapter is the importance of repeat and referral business. I can't stress enough the importance of learning how to capitalize on this part of your business. It's a goldmine full of cash that you need to discover. If you take anything from this chapter it should be the realization of how much opportunity lies within your previously sold guests. Start solid relationships with as many guests as possible, and continue to deliver the greatest customer service within your power. You now have the recipe for success; it's on you to implement it and make it happen.

# Chapter 4:
# The Power of the Telephone

*"A salesperson without a pen is like a soldier without a gun....A salesperson without a telephone is like a soldier without his brigade."*

Let's get better acquainted with your biggest tool in the business—the telephone. If you can't be strong on the phone and lock people down on appointments, you're finished. Throw in the towel now, because you'll never be better than average. Without your phone, you're nothing. The telephone is your strongest tool. How nice would it be to close a deal before you ever meet the guest, to be so strong on the phone that before your guest comes down to the dealership he or she already has one of your vehicles insured? It's very possible, but it all depends on how skilled you are on the phone.

The stronger you become, the easier it will be for you to lock down appointments and deals over the phone. Once you understand the importance of the telephone and you are able to master your phone skills, you will find selling cars to be a lot easier. Being able to sell over the phone allows you to prep your whole deal prior to meeting your guest. Being a master on the telephone will be your main advantage over all the average salespeople who neglect to take the time to practice and develop new skills.

I'm going to go over some of the most effective ways to take sales calls, book solid appointments, and get deals done over the phone, and I'm also going give you a number of tips that will help you elevate your game and get you to the next level in your salesmanship.

In a perfect world, everyone would have a 100 percent closing ratio on the phone, but they don't. I have a system that will get you as close to 100 percent as possible. Also, I'm going to show you how to handle the toughest sales calls so that you can capitalize on every opportunity you get. Once you become a master on the telephone, your volume is bound to increase.

# Sales Calls

Let's start this segment by talking about sales calls. As a salesperson, you rely on sales calls to generate appointments and leads, right? Well, every call is equivalent to an up (walk-in guest) or an Internet/credit lead. You can't waste any calls. Every call you take is a potential deal. You need to be able to take a call and navigate your way to a car deal, just like you do when you take an up and do a guest sheet. It's the same concept; the difference is this way you are working over the phone. Some salespeople will tell you they prefer sales calls instead of ups and vice versa. Why not master both? It could only equal one thing—more deals in the bank! Let's break this down. In order to have successfully taken a sales call, you need to have accomplished one of three things:

- Have a solid appointment booked

- Have done a preapproval over the phone

- Have set a follow-up call

When you take a sales call, it's typically a guest calling in requesting information about one or two vehicles that they have seen, more than likely on your website or wherever else you and your management team may have your inventory advertised. So from the guest's initial inquiry, you need to lock him or her down and start your sales process. In only two phone calls, you can find out the guest's needs and wants and then be able to transition into finance and availability.

I'm going to share with you a sales call script that was passed down to me by one of my greatest mentors. This script is tried, tested, and true. It is the ultimate script to use if you are looking to have the highest closing ratio at your store.

*Sales Call Script*

S: "Thanks for holding. This is Derek. Who am I speaking with, please?"
G: "Hello, my name is John."
S: "Hey, John. How are you doing today?"
G: "I'm doing well, and you?"
S: "I'm doing great. Thanks for asking. How can I help you, sir?"
G: "Yes, I'm calling about a 2010 Ford F150 I saw on your website."
S: "Perfect. Are you after that Ford F150 specifically, or were you just looking for a truck in that similar price range?"
G: "I was looking for that truck in particular."
S: "Awesome. What website are you looking at, and did you happen to have the stock number?"
G: "I am on your main website, and yes, the stock number is afb33333."
S: "Thanks a lot. This is what I'm going to do. I'm going to go and find out if that vehicle is still available, and at the same time I'm going to see if I can find a couple other trucks that are similar to that one. Can you grab a pen real quick? I need to give you some information."
G: "Yes, I have one."
S: "Great. My first name is D-e-r-e-k, and my last name is S-a-q-q-a. I'm also going to give you my personal cell phone number; that way you don't have to call the store anymore, and you can reach me directly on my cell. It's 7-8-0-5-5-5-4-4-4-4. Real quick—how do I spell your last name, John?"
G: "It's Johnson, J-o-h-n-s-o-n."
S: "And what's the best number for me to call you back on?"
G: "You can call my home. It's 7-8-0-6-6-6-5-5-5-5."
S: "Fantastic! Give me about five minutes. I'm going to get all that information for you, and I'll call you right back. If you have any other questions, just call my cell. If not, I'll talk to you right away."

That is the first part of the sales call. By answering the phone with "Thanks for holding. This is Derek. Who am I speaking with, please?" I am eliminating any objection to getting the guest's first name. How many times have you taken a sales call and asked for the guest's name, and he or she told you that he or she did not want to give you that information? By asking for it in your opening line, and not before you give them your first name, the caller will respond 100 percent of the time with his or her name, only because you've asked for it in a professional manner.

If you noticed, I never tried to book an appointment or do anything other than get all of the appropriate contact information that I would use to lead into my next call. Also, by not going for the appointment on the first call, you don't come across as a pushy salesperson. Most salespeople try to book an appointment right away without building any kind of relationship or getting the guest excited about any vehicles. The problem with that is that if you have not gotten your guest excited about any particular vehicles or you haven't built some form of relationship, the guest is less likely to show up to the appointment and will start avoiding your calls. It's important to build a relationship first and get your guest all the information that he or she has requested, and at that point, if the guest is excited and happy with the options you have given, then when you go to book the guest in for an appointment, he or she will be more likely to show up because you have made him or her comfortable, and the guest will feel like he or she knows who he or she is going to go see and what he or she is going to go look at.

Before I asked for all of the guest's contact information, I gave them all of my information first. The reason for that is I want to make sure the guest knows exactly who he or she is dealing with, and by giving them my cell phone number, this eliminates him or her from ever calling the store again. That way the guest can call you directly, and he or she will never get mixed up with another sales member. Also, by giving all of your information first, you are more likely to get all of the guest's information when you ask for it; it's less threatening for your guest to do so knowing that you just did the same.

During the initial call, you need to do some digging. Find out if the guest is only interested in the specific vehicle he or she inquired about or if he or she is open to similar vehicles in a similar price range. By asking that question, you are trying to open the door to all your inventory as opposed to just one vehicle; the more options you have to choose from, the more likely you are to land them on a unit and close the deal. More often than not, your guest will be open to different vehicles in a certain price range, but you have to ask. The second call is when you go in for the kill. I'll get there right away, but first, let's go back to part one where you asked if that was the particular vehicle the guest was looking for or not. Let me show you what to say if the guest answers differently.

S: "Perfect. Are you after a Ford F150 specifically, or were you just looking for a truck in that similar price range?"
G: "I'm just looking for a truck in that similar price range."
S: "OK, great! Well, we have lots of trucks in that price range. What I'll do is find out if that specific one you inquired about is still available, and at the same time I'll find a few comparable trucks that I think you would be interested in. Real quick—do you have a pen?"

Basically what you're doing is finding out what information the guest is looking for, and you are telling him or her that you will gather all that information and call back. This gives you a really good reason to get the guest's contact information, right? It also lets the guest know that you are prepared to work for him or her. Make sure you don't get sidetracked and forget to call the guest back within the five or ten minutes that you said you would. That's a great way to lose all credibility and decrease your chances of getting the guest through the doors.

Your second call is when you want to go in for the kill, and by kill I mean either book an appointment for your guest to come down to the dealership, do a preapproval over the phone, or have another follow-up call in place to accomplish one of the first two options. As long as the lead remains active, you have done your job. When you make the second call, you are calling to inform your guest that you have gotten all of his or her requested information. Now that you have done your job, you are entitled to start your sales process. Let me show you how your second call should go:

S: "Hey, John, how's it going? It's Derek returning your call. Listen, I got all that information you requested. That F150 you inquired about is still available, and it's actually sitting on my front lot right now. Not only that, I found a couple other F150s very similar to that one with right around the same kilometers as well. What part of town are you in right now?"
G: "I'm in the east side. I'm still at work."
S: "Awesome. What time do you finish work?"
G: "Five p.m."
S: "OK, so I actually have a couple openings this evening. What time did you want to come down and take a look at these trucks? We can go six fifteen p.m. or seven forty-five p.m."
G: "I can be there at seven forty-five p.m."
S: "Perfect. Do you still have that pen handy? I want to give you the address here. If you have any trouble finding the store, just call my cell."

OK, now let's say you go to make the second call, and you ask your guest what part of town he or she is in and the guest informs you that he or she is not from the city.

S: "Hey, John, how's it going? It's Derek returning your call. Listen, I got all that information you requested. That F150 you inquired about is still available, and it's actually sitting on my front lot right now. Not only that, I found a couple other F150s very similar to that one with right around the same kilometers as well. What part of town are you in right now?"
G: "Actually I'm calling from Calgary. I was planning on driving down this weekend."

S: That's perfect. If you're planning on driving a truck home the same day, the best thing for us to do is a no-obligation preapproval. I just need five more minutes of your time. I'm going to get some more basic information from you. I'll actually start working on your application today; that way when you drive down this weekend, I'll already have an approval in place for you. It's going to eliminate a lot of the waiting time for you."

G: "Sounds great."

So in that situation, when a guest is calling from out of town, always try to go for the preapproval. By doing so, you are taking the guest off the market. No one wants to have two or three different applications at different dealerships. They have no time for that. Customers want to deal with one honest salesperson or company that they can trust. If the guest declines the preapproval, though, it's OK. Don't force it on him or her. Pull back and book an appointment for the guest to come in on his or her next available day—the sooner the better.

Every guest is going to be different, but the call will go more or less the same. There will be some guests who are more eager and willing to come down to your dealership, and there will be other guests who want to get all the information they can from you to see if you can make it worth the trip for them. Follow this script so that you can differentiate what type of guest you have calling and what the best possible approach will be. This script isn't meant to be read word for word. During your sales call, you are going to have to engage in conversation and build relationships over the phone. It's OK if you go off script to build rapport; just make sure you are asking all the core questions and that you are doing it in sequence. Every time you pick up that phone remember what your ultimate purpose is. The ultimate purpose is to book an appointment, do a preapproval, or schedule a follow-up call so that you can book an appointment or do a preapproval.

> **Tip:** *The most effective way to utilize this script is to print it out. Memorize it and take turns role playing with another team member until you have it down pat. This way you won't buckle the next time your receptionist forwards a sales call to you. You will be ready and able to master it.*

## Preapprovals

A preapproval is when you get a credit application filled out with your guest so that you are able to submit the application to the bank and get the guest preapproved for a loan. Preapprovals are a great way to softly close a deal. The most effective times to offer preapprovals are over the phone or if you are having a hard time getting commitment from your in-house guests.

Wait for the opportune time to get a preapproval over the phone. When a guest tells you he or she is from out of town, a preapproval is a great way to save your guest time because you can get all the financing in order prior to him or her coming into the dealership; this eliminates a lot of waiting for your guest. If a guest hints to you that he or she has had some credit issues and is unsure about financing options, that's a great time to offer a preapproval as well. It will potentially save you and your guest some time by submitting the application prior to selecting a vehicle so that you can find out what lending institution will offer your guest the best rates and terms. Once you know how much money the banks are going to lend your guest, you can then pick a vehicle accordingly.

If you are having trouble closing an in-house guest (someone presently at your dealership) and you feel like he or she is starting to get cold feet and is just not sure if the payments you are offering will work, and you get the feeling that you are going to have to start pressuring him or her into signing a bill of sale, then offering a preapproval at this time is smart because you don't have to pressure your guest into sitting down in your finance office. You can tell them that while he or she goes home to think things over, you and your finance team will work on getting him or her the best rates possible so that when the guest does come back the next day you will be able to present him or her with exact rates, terms, and conditions. This gives you and your guest a fresh start the following day so that when he or she comes in, you can start off right where you left off, only this time you already have an approval in place and your finance team is ready to sign the financing contracts with no waiting period for your guest. The guest will then be in and out in of your dealership driving away in his or her new vehicle.

Taking that approach sometimes works out better for you as well. There are times you will want to close the deal so badly because you have so much time invested with your guest that you will try so hard to get your guest to sign a bill of sale. At this point, you are usually an hour or two, if not more, into your deal, depending on how many vehicles the guest needed to test drive before committing or how many obstacles you had to overcome to get him or her to the negotiation stage. You finally get your guest to sign the bill of sale, and he or she thinks it's over, only to have you tell your guest that he or she now has to sit in the lounge and wait for your finance team to start the financing process, which at times, can take several hours. This can become overwhelming for your guest, and the amount of hours and waiting time spent in your dealership will deteriorate your guest's excitement and experience. Splitting the process up into two separate days will eliminate a lot of that frustration from your guests. Every dealership has its own process, so those types of decisions regarding waiting times will more than likely be decided by your management. However, I'm sure your management team will be able to make the most educated decisions in those types of situations. It's just something for you to watch for.

Can't get a deposit over the phone? It's OK. Get insurance. A good way to secure a car deal is to make a request to your guest to get the vehicle that he or she is looking to finance insured. Getting insurance on a vehicle prior to having your guest come down is better than a deposit. It's the highest form of commitment. The best way to go about it is to inform your guest that the banks will need to see a copy of the insurance to make sure that he or she is insurable. This is also another way to secure the loan, because if someone can't get insurance, the banks won't finance that person. You can also inform your guest that the approval is conditional subject to proof of insurability. If you sell this hard enough, your guest will go ahead and insure the vehicle prior to even road testing it just to confirm his or her approval.

Ask your guest if he or she has an insurance company that he or she is currently dealing with, and if the guest does, that's great. If not, offer to set your guest up with one of your insurance brokers. It's always good to have a couple of different insurance brokers who give you competitive quotes. Sometimes an insurance quote can make or break a car deal. Also, getting your guests in the habit of setting up insurance and offering them help to set it up saves them time, and more importantly, it's far more convenient for them to have you set the insurance up. It's one less obstacle they have to consider and deal with during their purchase.

# Building Relationships

*"The stronger you are as an individual, the stronger your relationships will be as a whole."*

Building relationships over the telephone prior to ever meeting a guest face-to-face is one of the greatest advantages you will gain when it comes time to sell a car. By building a solid relationship over the phone, you are creating a foundation for your sale. You will be more prepared to deal with your guest when he or she comes down to the store because you already know what the guest is looking for, and you also already have a taste of the guest's personality, and vice versa, so there isn't that need to gain an initial perception on your first encounter or that need for a quick character evaluation on your initial meet and greet.

When you are dealing with someone over the phone, you want to make sure you get all the information you need from that person in order to make his or her experience in your store great and quick. When you are dealing with guests over the telephone, you want to come across as confident and professional. Your guests need to feel like they are in the best hands possible. Reassuring them of that and also staying true to your word are two things that are very important if you want to earn a reputation as a reputable salesperson. If you want to be the best, you need to be organized and responsible.

One of the biggest mistakes I see over and over again is the promise of returning a call to a guest and then forgetting to make that call. That is the ultimate sin. There is no excuse for it, and no guest will tolerate it. There are way too many tools and reminders out there for you to say you forgot to call back because you got busy or sidetracked. If you have to put a reminder on a sticky note or on your mobile phone, do so. The stronger you become, the more business you will generate, and in turn, the busier you will be. As you excel, your time management skills will have to excel with you. The best way to avoid getting caught in a position where you forget to fulfill your promise to return a guest's call is to get yourself in the habit of putting the onus on your guest to call you back at his or her preferred time. So if you know you and your guest need to make contact tomorrow, then as you're talking to him or her, just ask what time he or she can call you back, and reiterate the fact that you will be waiting for the call. Put the responsibility on your guest. Doing so also acts as a form of trust between you and your guest because you are leaving yourself vulnerable to him or her by placing the next point of contact in his or her hands. This shows the guest that you are professionally working together toward one common goal: consulting your guest into a smart vehicle purchase. This way the phone calls aren't always one-sided either.

If you are looking to develop solid business relationships with your guests, you need to work on your reputation. It is just as important to build these solid relationships with your fellow sales members and management team as well. In order to up your game and join the big leagues, you need to tap into all areas of opportunities. Building great relationships with your guests will open doors to repeat and referral business. Building solid relationships with your team will open doors for you as well; if you are perceived as a solid, reliable, and dependable individual, you will become, by nature, the store's go-to person when an important job needs to be executed.

Picture yourself from your guests' point of view and from your coworkers' point of view. What would they say about you?

Would they say that you are trustworthy?

Would they say that you are honest?

Would they say that you are willing to go the extra mile in order to give your guests an extraordinary car-buying experience?

Would they say that you are dependable?

Would they say that you are reliable?

Would they say you are knowledgeable in all areas of your field?

Asking yourself these questions and then answering them from your guests' and coworkers' perspectives will give you a really good idea as to whether or not you feel like you are doing everything in your power to be the best at what you do or if you are coasting by as an average salesperson who's content with being average and has no desire to excel and actually make a name for himself or herself in the industry. If you answered yes to all of the above questions, then you and I are on the same page. Take a few minutes and really let these question soak in. It's crucial to understand how you believe other people view your character. Once you feel like you have a good idea of where you stand, it's now time to ask yourself, *Do I want to grow and develop my skills so I can be the best at what I do? Do I want to be known as trustworthy and reliable among my fellow team members and my valued customers?* The obvious answer to those two questions is **yes**.

Use this last exercise as a constant reminder that people are being influenced by your actions every single day. What kind of influence do you want to have on them? Remember that everything you say and do is a direct reflection of your character, so always say and do things that reflect how you would like to be looked upon. It's very rare that someone can truthfully answer yes to all of the above questions. As long as you can truthfully tell yourself that you are working on all these different areas, then you are on your way to becoming a champion.

## Phone Tips

Here are a few tips for you to try out that will help you master the phone. These are everyday tools for you to use. Try them out and see how effective they are for you.

1. **Always check your messages, and always call your guests back now, not later.**

If you miss a call from a guest, call him or her back as soon as possible. If you neglect to call your guest back, he or she will feel like you aren't professional and that you don't really care about him or her. Don't avoid a guest who is having issues with his or her vehicle. If your guest is having issues, get your manager involved and deal with those issues now. The longer you go without returning a guest's call, the more upset your guest will become and the harder it will be for you to diffuse the situation. This is a big one when it comes to your personal customer service. If you aren't serving your customer, you will lose all chances of repeat and referral business. The more advanced in sales you become, the more you will understand the importance of repeats and referrals.

2. **Set up a professional voice mail without stating the company you work for and your position.**

When you're setting up your voice mail, try not to state your position or company. Just keep your message quick and simple.

"Hello. You have reached the confidential voice mail of _____. Unfortunately I missed your call. Please leave me your name and number, and I will call you back as soon as possible. Thanks and have a great day."

There is no need to state your position on your voice mail because if you are a strong salesperson, you need to be able to play different roles and have different personas depending on each guest. As much as you are a salesperson, you are also a credit specialist as well as an Internet manager and also part of your company's business development center. There are multiple roles you can take on when you are on the sales floor. Here's another reason for not leaving your company name on your voice mail. As much as I hate to say it, some guests will avoid you if they know you are representing a car dealership. By not exposing your company on your voice mail, then when a guest calls you back and you miss his or her call, the guest will hear your voice mail and leave a message, the whole time not knowing who you are. This will keep your guests interested to find out why you are calling them and why they are calling you back. At least by getting them on the line you get an opportunity to entice them into coming down to your dealership.

3. **Leave a great-news message.**

When you are leaving a voice mail for a guest, make it short and sweet. It doesn't matter what guest you're calling or why you're calling. Your call should only go one way.

> *"Hey, Mr. Customer. This is _____ calling. I need you to call me back ASAP. I have some great news to share with you! My phone number is_____, and once again, my name is _____, and I'm calling with great news. My number again is _____. Thank you so much! I'm looking forward to hearing from you!"*

This message is quick and simple. Think about it. Who doesn't want to hear great news? By leaving a great-news message all the time, I guarantee you that your returned calls will increase by a landslide. Reverse the situation for a second and just think of how you would feel if a random person called you personally and told you they had great news for you and asked for you to call them back right away? Your first reaction would always be "Hmmm…I wonder what the great news is?" Then you would call them back, right? Give it a shot. You will have everyone wondering who you are and what kind of great news you have for them.

4. **Never speak in monotone. Always have energy and character in your voice.**

You are not a robot! You are a human being. When a customer sets out to buy a vehicle, he or she wants to buy from someone he or she can like and trust. This comes down to your attitude and character. Don't be a bore, have lots of energy in your voice, and show your character over the phone. Don't be a Debby Downer over the phone. If you're not excited and you're speaking in a quiet voice, then you are not doing your job. People don't want to deal with people who are dull and boring. If you are reading off a script while you are talking to someone on the phone, your guest will pick up on that. Memorize your scripts and pitches so you can speak in confidence. Get your guests excited to buy a vehicle from you. You should be hanging up every call feeling like you just gave the person on the other line the best news of his or her life. Your excitement and attitude are what will dictate every sale you make.

5.  **Text, text, text, and text.**

Text messages are king. Any time you have an opportunity to text your guest, go for it. It's just as effective as a phone call, if not more effective. Sometimes guests are busy, or they are at work and it's harder for them to pick up their phone. If you send them a text, it's easy for them to read your text and respond to you. These days more and more people are getting more comfortable with text messages as opposed to phone calls. Texts are quicker, and they give the other person the ability to respond at his or her own pace. A text message is less threatening than a phone call.

6.  **Put the onus on your guest to call you back instead of you calling him or her back.**

If you are the type of individual who always falls victim to not returning calls to your guests, this tip will do wonders for you. Calling your guests back on time is a golden rule in this business. If you have too much on your plate and you just can't seem to put a system in place that helps you stay in control of calling guests back, then the next time you are talking to one of your guests and you are about to set up a follow-up call for the following day, whether it's for an update on the guest's vehicle or an update to let the guest know if his or her financing went through, then instead of telling the guest that you will call him or her the following afternoon, ask the guest what his or her schedule is like tomorrow and tell him or her to call you back on his or her lunch break or on an agreed-upon time. By training yourself to get into this habit of getting your guests to call you back, you don't have to worry about calling them back, and you can just sit back and wait for their call instead. This way a guest can never get upset with you for not calling him or her back because the guest is the one who committed to calling you. This habit isn't meant to be used on fresh leads (customers who you just started talking to, or unsold guests who you are still working on getting into the store and selling them a car.) This habit is meant to be used on guests who you already have an established relationship with, like repeat guests, referrals, and freshly sold guests.

7. **Never think twice about making a follow-up call.**

Remember that every guest you talk to, either sold or unsold, is just a customer. Everyone you talk to is just another opportunity to get a deal and potentially build a business relationship with. If you are doing a follow-up call, don't fear a negative reaction. What's the worst that can happen? Well, I'll tell you. Absolutely nothing! I have made more follow-up calls than I can ever dream of counting, and the worst thing that has ever happened to me was a harsh rejection. I've listened to rejection after rejection, waiting to get positive responses. Some people are open to listening to you, and others are not. The more you get rejected, the more likely you are to get a positive response from a guest. Getting rejected is part of the game. You can't sell cars if you have a fear or rejection.

8. **Always do business on your cell phone rather than the work line.**

Try and get all your guests to call you on your cell phone. To take a sales call on the work line is normal. Get in the habit of making calls from your cell and giving all your guests your cell number. You will miss fewer calls, and at the same time your guests will never get mixed up with another sales member. Doing so eliminates any confusion between you, your guests, and other sales staff. Also, if you're usually in and out of the dealership, it will be more convenient for you to take calls on your cell.

9. **Always appear busy.**

People want to deal with people who are busy. The busier you are, the better you are. So it's never a bad thing to come across as being very busy. When you are dealing with guests who are trying to book appointments, tell them that you have a few appointments that day but that you only have two available spots. Give them two different times to choose from. If you can understand and learn how to create commotion and the appearance of being very busy, you will change the way customers respond to you.

10. **"No problem, sir" and "Yes, ma'am."**

As a salesperson, you can never forget to be respectful and show a little gratitude. When you are talking to any guest, remember that he or she is the one who allows you to live the life you do and put food on your table. Always use the words "sir" and "ma'am" unless the guest tells you otherwise. Politely addressing others is one of the highest forms of respect. Refer to your guest as sir or ma'am. If not, make sure you call a guest by his or her first name. It's a little more personable, and it shows that you guys can be on a friend level as well. It also shows tons of professionalism on your end.

Practice these tips one at a time, and start to utilize them on an everyday basis. They are going to help you look and sound professional in the eyes of all your guests and coworkers. They will help you stay organized and stay one step ahead of everyone else.

# Booking Appointments

*"You are only as solid as your appointments."* – *John Kalogeras*

A big part of the game is being able to book solid appointments with guests to get them in the door. Sounds easy enough, but how many times have you booked an appointment with a guest and you got all excited and prepared only to have your guest not show up? It's happened to all of us, some more than others. It has nothing to do with luck or coincidence. It has everything to do with your phone skills and how solid and professional you are when you are talking to people on the phone.

Let's get one thing straight. If you can't speak and sound professional over the phone, people won't respect you and your abilities to help them out. So if you are talking to a guest over the phone, trying to book him or her in for an appointment, but you are stuttering and mumbling and you can't really answer the guest's questions and your primary focus is just booking a time and date with him or her so that you can go show your manager that you booked an appointment for the day, odds are the guest you booked that appointment with won't feel inclined or obligated to come down to your dealership. You need to work hard and listen to what your guest is telling you he or she needs in order to make a vehicle purchase. Then you need to entice your guest enough so that he or she is excited and committed to you so that when the guest books an appointment with you, he or she can actually say, "Hey, this salesperson really went the extra mile to get us all the information we requested." At that point the guest will feel obligated to come down for his or her appointment because you have put in the time for him or her. You have proven that you are professional and able to help him or her, so out of respect for you and your professionalism, your guest will give you an opportunity to earn his or her business in return.

Here are some bad phone habits that you should look out for and avoid at all times.

- *Chewing gum.* It's disrespectful and unprofessional to chew gum in person or over the phone—especially if you chew like a horse.

- *Speaking in monotone.* If you speak in monotone, you show no character, and your words come out as very scripted. Without a personality, you can't sell cars.

- *Speaking in a low voice.* Wake up! Get excited! How do you expect to excite someone enough to make his or her biggest purchase in life, aside from a home, if you sound like you are half dead or sleeping? Selling is about putting on a show and moving people into buying a vehicle. Remember, you are the one driving the sales bus from beginning to end, but you need to make sure your guest doesn't try and get off the bus too early.

- *Not listening.* Shut up and listen. This sale isn't about you; it's about your guest and his or her needs and wants. Let your guest do the talking. It's your job to listen and help him or her make an educated decision.

- *Cutting someone off while he or she is speaking.* This is a really great way to offend someone. If someone is talking about something, let that person finish; don't cut them off. When you cut someone off, this shows that you don't care about what he or she has to say and that you feel that your voice or opinion is more important.

- *Too much verbal diarrhea.* Don't talk yourself out of a car deal. Listen to what your guest has to say, and then respond accordingly. Sometimes less is more. Be direct and to the point. Try to avoid going off subject; if you go too far, it may be difficult to get back to the point.

- *Foul language.* Swearing is never a positive thing. Try to avoid swearing because it's a sign of unprofessionalism. If you swear over the phone, there is very good chance that you will offend the person on the other end of the line.

- *Loud background.* Avoid taking a call in a loud area. You need to be able to listen and understand your guest when he or she speaks, without any distractions. Also, it can become frustrating for your guest to have to listen to loud noise in the background. You work at a dealership, not a zoo. The most effective way to make calls is to seclude yourself in a quiet area; that way you can get in the zone and handle your calls appropriately.

In this business, you need to rely on appointments to sell cars. Statistically speaking, you should be closing 50 percent of your appointments. So for every two appointments you book, you should be closing one of them. Do the math. One appointment per day for thirty days should result in an average of fifteen deals. So your goal should be to book at least two solid appointments a day to average around the thirty-deal mark. It's not as easy as it sounds, but it's a great target. These appointments can be generated from sales calls, showroom walk-ins, Internet leads, repeat and referral business, service guests, be-backs, and networking your own business through sources like Kijiji and self-advertising.

Think about that statistic, and then think about your day-to-day operations and ask yourself how hard would it really be to book two appointments a day? If your typically only booking one appointment a day right now, then you need to generate another form of business so that you can go from one appointment a day to two. Don't stop there. Once you can network your way to two appointments per day, start working toward averaging three appointments per day, and keep it going. Look for different forms of networking, and find something that works effectively for you so you can capitalize on deals. A great salesperson is also a great networker. The deals aren't just going to fall from the sky. You need to generate your own business. These extra steps are what will take you from average and send you on your way to the top of the board.

## Effective Communication

Being able to communicate effectively will play a big role in your success. The key part to this is always having clarity between all parties. Whether it's between you and your guest or you and your finance manager or sales manager, communication is key. To run a well-oiled machine, all the parts have to be active and working together in order to do or create what they were designed to do. So to properly handle a deal from front to back, you need to rely on the communication between you, your guest, your finance manager, and your sales manager because all parties play a role in the complete execution of every deal.

Having proper communication with all of your guests eliminates any type of doubt that your guests may have about you or your product. If your guests have any questions, be sure to answer them properly and reiterate the fact that you guys are still on the same page. Never deflect a question without having any intention of answering it. You may deflect questions in order to give an explanation before answering it. If a guest asks you a question and you neglect to answer it, that's when the guest starts to doubt you and your professionalism, leading your guest to question your motive. Having full clarity on all your deals will reduce your tube ratio (deals that unwind after the guest signs a bill of sale) because your guest will have a full understanding of his or her purchase in regard to the vehicle and financing.

It's just as important to have the same communication with your finance manager. If you have discussed something with your guest that you think your finance manager would benefit from knowing, make sure you communicate what you and your guest have spoken about to your finance manager. It could be warranty options or financing rates and terms. Whatever it is, always tee up your finance department to any conversations you've had about finance products and terms. If you can, try to leave all the finance talk for your finance team. Many guests want to discuss rates and terms over the phone prior to coming down. If you disclose that information over the phone, not only are you breaking a privacy act between merchant and customer information, but you are also putting all your cards on the table at the wrong time.

Let's just say, for example, that a guest tells you that he or she wants to know his or her interest rate before coming down to the dealership. You can do one of two things. You can tell the guest his or her interest rate over the phone and run the risk of your guest telling you that the interest rate your dealership is offering is too high and leaving them with an opportunity to shop your rate at a different dealership. Or the best route for you to take in this situation is to simply explain to your guest that, due to privacy acts, you cannot disclose that information over the phone, and at the same time tell the guest that his or her interest rate will be dependent on the year and kilometers of the vehicle he or she chooses. Your guest will understand the circumstances because you have justified, with reason, why you can't disclose that information. Not only that, you have explained to the guest that the interest rate hasn't been established because no vehicle has been chosen yet. This way you can still get your guest through the doors, with the intention of starting your selling process and getting him or her excited about a particular vehicle. Once you have the guest sold on a vehicle that they really want, the interest rate becomes secondary. You now have the opportunity to close the guest on payments and rates while he or she is at the dealership and in a buying mood. It is 100 percent more effective to close rates and payments face-to-face while the guest is in house rather than over the phone. If you try to do these tasks over the phone, you will get way less commitment because the guest is less obligated to make a decision. Your guest can easily tell you that he or she will think about it and call you back.

Use the phone to your advantage and take extra time to develop your phone skills because they are your greatest asset. You have the power to control all of your deals, but you will need your phone to do so. Proper communication and proper delegation over the telephone will lead to proper execution. Practice all of the tips and tools I have given you, and start making an impact every time you pick up your telephone.

Start implementing these tips one by one and see what works best for you. Once you start utilizing some of my tips and tools, your numbers will go up and your appointments will become tighter and tighter. You will be on your way to becoming a pro. Your phone is your best friend and will account for a huge part of your business, so don't take its importance lightly.

# Chapter 5:
# The World Wide Web

Let's get acquainted with the World Wide Web. We find ourselves in a time where anything and everything is available to us on the Internet. The Internet is a massive source of information that allows the public to research anything they can possibly imagine. It's a wonderful source of information that can come in handy while dealing with virtually any situation.

So what does that mean for us salespeople? It means that we need to be aware of and in tuned with what kind of vehicle information is available to our guests. It also means that if we are going to stay one step ahead of the game, we need to be able to embrace the Internet and use it to our advantage.

Due to the massive amount of information on the Internet, the general public has information on new car rebates and incentives. They also have access to MSRP pricing (manufacturer's suggested retail price), Black Book values, Blue Book values, and comparable pricing on used vehicles within any market. There are even how-to videos on how to approach car dealerships when looking to purchase a vehicle. All this information is relevant to you and your business. Being aware of this kind of information will give you the competitive edge against any kinds of objections that can be formed through misinformed Internet websites and videos. It's not a bad thing to have all of this information exposed to the public. It's only a bad thing if you aren't aware of it and get caught hitting a roadblock because you don't have a rebuttal for a guest who presents a concern or question that is formulated from information found on the Internet.

Embrace the Internet and use it to your advantage. How can you take the information that's out there and make it beneficial to you and your business? I'm not going to get into marketing and website strategies. That's a whole other book on its own. I'm talking about what customers see and do prior to making a vehicle purchase and also what we as salespeople can do to be ready for these customers and stay ahead of the game.

Let's start by viewing the customer's perspective. Understanding the buyer's angle will help you take the most effective approach when dealing with guests on day to day. What steps do buyers take when they initially set out to purchase a new vehicle? Have you personally ever purchased a vehicle from a car dealership or been involved with someone close to you who has? Do you remember the experience? How often do you, as a consumer, seek out to make a purchase, not necessarily a vehicle purchase, but any purchase where you started out by shopping online? What did you automatically search for—quality, easy-to-navigate websites or best price?

Over 90 percent of car buyers, at one point in time throughout their purchase, research cars online before they buy. Most often, consumers start their vehicle search online. That is the majority. So as a salesperson in the car sales industry, it's a great idea to know what consumers are looking to find online, as well as what they are finding. Knowing this information will help you get a deeper understanding of what to look out for and how to navigate your guests through their purchase. This knowledge will also help you in identifying hot buttons when dealing with your guests.

## Understanding New Car Buyers

Let's start with the new car buyer. A new car buyer probably starts off by going online and doing some research on dealer specials as well as rebates and incentives. A new car buyer already has a general idea of what he or she is looking to buy in regard to type of vehicle. If the buyer wants a sedan, he or she will research a few different ones. The buyer will research those options and safety features that he or she would like to have in the new vehicle that are in line with the buyer's desired price point. The buyer will generate a good idea of what sedans he or she intends to test drive based on the information he or she has collected from different dealer websites. It's the same concept for someone looking for SUVS, minivans, trucks, etc. Once the buyer feels like he or she has narrowed down his or her search, then over 50 percent of guests prefer to just walk into a dealership as opposed to inquiring online.

> *Tip: A great question to ask your guests is "Have you guys ever been on our website?" and "Have you guys gotten any information online yet?" Ask those questions during you're initial qualifying step. The answers will let you know if the people in front of you have been doing their homework or not.*

Why is this information so important to you as a salesperson? Well, if you are in the new car market selling new vehicles, you will always have an advantage over your guests by knowing what types of rebates and incentives your manufacturer is offering at any given time. That should go without saying. If you don't have a clue about the special offers and rebates your dealership has to offer, you are sure to lose all credibility and control of your deals because you're less prepared than the buyer. Once you find yourself in that hole, it's very hard to climb out of it. Always remember that the consumers you are dealing with more than likely know all of that information prior to walking into your dealership after researching it online. They may not always accumulate accurate information, but they have a general idea of what can or cannot be offered by the dealer.

Don't stop there. Knowing what your specific manufacturer has to offer in regards to deals, promotions, rebates, and incentives is great, but you also need to know what the competition around you is offering as well. That's when you should feel like you are definitely staying ahead of the game. You need to be able to compare your offerings with other manufacturers' offerings. It's always great if you are around to help your guests compare deals. You can be sure to find a way to make your deal reign supreme over the next dealers' deals. Having all this information on your competitors will also help you eliminate any unforeseen objections throughout your sale if a guest won't commit to your product without checking out a comparable vehicle at a different manufacturer. It's one more angle for you to take by being able to present what the other manufacturers are offering on their comparable vehicles and explain why and how you can make your deal sweeter.

Having all this knowledge in your toolbox will help you be more professional and close more deals. Everybody likes to deal with a salesperson who knows what he or she is talking about. You will make your guests feel like you are the obvious choice to buy from based off your awareness and expertise.

> *Reminder: You never want to bash or bad-mouth your competition. Never say anything negative about a competitor. In fact, it doesn't hurt to say positive things about competitors. Your competitors can be a great group of people with great products and services. You just need to show how your products and services are greater and stronger than the rest! Any negativity throughout a sale can turn your guests off and get them out of the buying mood.*

New car buyers are looking to find value. You need to be able to present the value of yourself, your company, and your product throughout your sale in order for you to turn a shopper into a buyer. Fly straight when it comes to pricing and all other information. Don't fall into the stereotype and be a "sleazy salesperson" with your guests. Be upfront about everything, and put all your cards on the table at the right time. Genuinely try and help every guest have a great experience, and help them make the most educated decision when it comes to his or her vehicle purchase.

## Understanding Used Car Buyers

Now let's talk about the used car buyer. A used car buyer is primarily going to focus on exact vehicles that he or she thinks would be nice and affordable based on appearance and price point. The advantage used car buyers have over new car buyers is wider vehicle selection and price points. Fifteen thousand dollars can buy a sedan, SUV, truck, a nice sports car, or even a Mercedes Benz. The dynamic of years and kilometers will allow a used car buyer with a $15,000 budget to have all types of choices when it comes to selecting his or her new preowned vehicle. It now becomes a matter of what's more important to the buyer—style and appearance or year and kilometers. And these depend on the individual. Another advantage to buying a preowned vehicle is the fact that the lump sum of the depreciation factor has already taken place. That doesn't mean that preowned vehicles have stopped depreciating; it just means that the individual who purchased the vehicle new from the manufacturer already took the biggest hit.

As a used car salesperson, you really need to pay attention to what kind of information consumers can find online about used cars. The used car market in the eyes of the consumers can be very influenced through stories and bad experiences. The used car market is where the phrase "Buyer beware" really comes to light. After so many bad experiences about so-called lemons being sold and these stories being uploaded onto the Internet and read by consumers, many consumers really have their guard up and their trust level is down prior to walking into a preowned car dealership.

But the facts are the facts. As a salesperson selling used vehicles, make sure you have a reputable dealership that stands behind you. Some things will never change, and that's the need to have a great reputation in your community and in your city. When you are selling preowned vehicles, make sure your guests know that you and your dealership's reputation is what matters most. It's best to convey these types of things through real customer testimonials—real stories of how you and your dealership have been situations where you had unsatisfied guests and what you guys did to make things up to them. Customer service is a huge selling point for used car buyers. They want to know that you as a dealer will take recourse (within reason) if, for some reason, they feel like their newly acquired preowned vehicle turns out to be a "lemon." Don't be afraid to let a guest know that getting a lemon does happen. Don't hide the fact that you have had unsatisfied guests in the past or that you have had guests come back with complaints about their preowned vehicles. It's not all sunshine and lollipops in the used car world. Believe me when I tell you it would make everyone's life a lot easier if it were.

You need to create a mutual understanding of the business between you and the used car buyer. The facts are that you are selling preowned vehicles, and for the most part, the majority of consumers leave 100 percent satisfied. There will always be situations where a preowned vehicle leaves the lot and doesn't pan out to be as mechanically sound as it appeared to be during the initial dealer inspection. In that situation, all you're guest needs is peace of mind that you as his or her sales consultant and preferred dealer will not leave the guest high and dry if he or she finds themselves in that situation.

What does a used car buyer do when he or she initially sets out to buy a car, and why isn't the person buying new?

Well, for the most part, we covered the two main reasons why used car buyers buy used as opposed to new. The first reason is the depreciation aspect, and second reason is the limited choices within a given budget. What else drives a consumer to go used rather than new, you ask?

How about people who have had some credit issues in the past? It doesn't take much to ruin a credit score. If a person screws over a cell phone company, this will damage that person's credit. If someone can't keep up with his or her credit card payments, this will damage that person's credit. If someone "voluntarily" repossesses his or her vehicle, this will damage that person's credit. If someone has gone through a bankruptcy in the past, this will obviously damage that person's credit. There are many individuals who have gone through tough times in the past and have found themselves in a rebuilding phase in their lives. These are the individuals who will automatically drive themselves toward the used car market to try and get financed for a vehicle.

Every new car advertisement out there, whether it's on the radio, in a magazine, on the Internet, or in a newspaper advertises zero percent financing or 1.9 percent financing (these are low interest rates that can't be offered on used car programs), which will always automatically attract buyers with established credit who believe they can qualify for such rates. A consumer with poor credit history wouldn't see, read, or hear a new car advertisement and feel like he or she would qualify for those types of rates or feel like those types of ads were calling his or her name—which is not a false thought. For the most part, it's true. You will never hear a new car advertisement that promotes bad credit history. So what is happening through the power of advertisement is the split between buyers with established credit and buyers with poor credit. The new car industry will always advertise to attract individuals with good established credit because those are the individuals who can afford and qualify for the new car products and services. The used car market specifically advertises to attract buyers with past credit issues because it that car purchase can affect these buyers in a positive way. Thanks to the massively wide range of vehicles and financing options available in the used car market, it's easier for the used car buyer and the used car seller to come to terms on a deal. The used car buyer isn't focused on rebates and incentives. The used car buyer is focused on what type of interest rate he or she will qualify for and what kind of payments he or she can be offered on his or her desired vehicle.

So as a used car seller, you need to focus more on wants versus needs, qualifications, and, most importantly, budget. You need to be able to sit down with every used car buyer and pinpoint what's most important to him or her in regard to type of vehicle (car, truck, SUV, crossover, and minivans), along with options, and then align those items with the buyer's budget (monthly payments). Then from there, you need to find out the buyer's credit situation to see if he or she can qualify for what he or she is looking for or if the buyer will need to compromise for the first year just to get back on track in the "credit world." The better you get at understanding this strategy, the better you will become at closing more used car deals. This is where your skills as a salesperson will come into play. You use the same selling principles in regard to finding hot buttons and have a great attitude toward any given situation to help drive you closer to the finish line. Because no matter who you have in front of you, you can't forget that you are still selling something. Being aware of an individual's situation and being able to explain to that person why he or she is where he or she is and how you can help him or her get closer to an ultimate goal or desired vehicle is what will separate you from the average salesperson.

Tip: When dealing with guests who have poor credit history, never tell them that they can't get what they want right after your initial qualifying step. Always tell your guests that you and your finance team are going to do everything in your power to get them the best possible financing options. This will eliminate any doubt from your guests after they leave your store and will stop them from shopping a different dealer at the same time. At the same time, you are pushing your sales process to the next step by giving yourself an opportunity to switch your guests the next time they come to your dealership. Once you get the best possible approval, bring your guest back in and put the onus on the bank as to why he or she can't qualify for exactly what he or she wants. Your chances of closing that deal while your guest is back in your dealership are greater than if you would have told your guest right from the get-go that he or she had no chance of getting exactly what he or she wanted. You now have the opportunity to show your guest his or her next-best options.

# Internet Sales Department

*"The quicker the response, the greater the first impression for an Internet buyer."*

The Internet sales department is a great place for a salesperson who is looking to take his or her career one step higher. In most cases, the income is higher than in regular sales because if you find yourself working in the Internet department, you're volume will automatically increase due to the amount of Internet leads you receive. A lot of dealers will pick one or two capable individuals to run the whole department, while other dealers will choose to split the leads among all their sales staff. It all depends on their results. In a lot of cases, the Internet sales department is accountable for over 50 percent of the dealership's overall monthly gross and volume. So it's in management's best interest to make sure that its strongest team members are running this department so that they can capitalize on its full earning potential.

What does it take to be an effective member of an Internet department?

Internet sales is a lot like regular sales. The only difference is that the leads come to you online as opposed to you taking regular walk-in traffic or sales calls, etc. It sounds pretty easy, doesn't it?

Well, it all depends on you as an individual. If I were to walk into any dealership, on any sales floor, and pull all the sales members to the side and ask them by a show of hands who would want to exclusively sell off of Internet leads and who would prefer to exclusively sell off of sales calls and walk-in traffic, I guarantee you that in every situation there would be close to a 50 percent split between the people who want to sell from the Internet leads and the people who want to sell from the sales floor. There is a reason for that. The reason is, although sales members who are part of the Internet department appear to have it easier than the front-line sales staff because they sell more cars and earn higher wages and have all their leads gift wrapped and given to them via e-mail right onto their computer screen, there is a lot more to their job than most people give them credit for.

It takes a lot of following up and organization skills to be great at selling cars in the Internet department. There are times where these individuals have to follow up on guests for weeks and even months before they get an opportunity to close a deal. To work in this department, one needs to be able to answer e-mails promptly from work or from home, with no exceptions. There is a saying in the car business: "Time kills deals!" Well, in the Internet department, amplify that statement by ten, then press send!

When it comes time to responding to an Internet lead, you have no time. The second a lead comes through, you are on the ticker. The longer it takes for you to respond to a lead, the less likely you are to turn it into a car deal.

Internet shoppers are online doing their research. They are collecting as much information as they can, and they eventually get to a point where they feel the need to make an inquiry about something that they aren't clear on. It could be the price, clarification on extra fees, how to take the next step from the website toward making an actual purchase, or even something as simple as arranging a time to come down and take a vehicle on a test drive.

Regardless of what these customers are inquiring, you better be around and ready to respond with an answer. This is the first point of contact between you and your Internet prospect. Put yourself in the customer's seat. If you are online shopping on a dealer website and you decided to make an inquiry, how long would you wait for a response before you felt like you were never going to get one? Five minutes? Thirty minutes? One hour? Two hours? Overnight? Well, as each minute goes by, as a consumer, you slowly lose interest, and, more importantly, you lose hope with that dealership and you will more than likely continue to shop online and find yourself on the next dealer's website, entering another inquiry and waiting for a response. Now that website happens to respond within minutes of your inquiry. Out of the two websites, which one of them gains the most credibility right from the get-go? The second one would appear to be the clear choice. They were prompt with their response and gave you a sense that they are highly organized. An Internet shopper is not going to wait around for you to respond; they will continue to inquire because they are already engaged in their online car shopping and are excited enough to take the next step. If you wait longer than a few minutes to respond, you run the risk of allowing a customer to make several inquiries. By responding immediately, you keep the customer engaged with you and your company, allowing you a fair opportunity to navigate yourself into a car deal.

By now, you should understand the importance of a quick response, so let's move on and look into the main types of inquiries that come through online and how to deal with them.

*General Vehicle Inquires*

Many Internet leads are generated by consumers who are trying to get information about any particular vehicle. People inquire to find out what types of options a certain vehicle may have. If it's an inquiry on a used vehicle, a lot of the questions will be about the history and condition of the used vehicle.

A vehicle inquiry lead will look a lot like this:

joeyporter@hdot.com
"Hello. I was wondering whether or not this vehicle (stock#afa33333) has been in any accidents? Can you tell me if it has heated seats? Also, would you be able to tell me the engine size, and last off, how many car seats can it handle?"

dereksaqqa@go.ca
"Good afternoon, Joey! Thanks for taking an interest in our 2010 Dodge Durango (stock# afa33333). I will do my best to answer all of your questions and help you throughout your vehicle purchase! To start off, if you go onto our website gocars@gocars.ca, you will find a carproof report attached to every one of our vehicles. I have already reviewed the carproof report on the specific vehicle that you inquired about and found out that it has no previous damage records found. The vehicle is local, and by the looks of it, it has only been registered to one owner prior to our store purchasing it. This particular Durango does not come equipped with heated seats because the SE model does not offer that option. Were you specifically looking to purchase a new vehicle that came with heated seats? The engine size in this particular vehicle is a 3.6 liter V6. That gets thirteen miles per gallon. Last but not least, I just went outside to look at the vehicle, and I confirmed that it is able to hold up to three car seats at any given time. What is it about this particular vehicle that piqued your interest?"

Now, the key is to be able to take this simple vehicle inquiry and turn it into an appointment. It's a lot like filling out a guest sheet with a regular walk-in customer. You need to gather up all the requested information. Make sure you respond with answers to all of the questions asked by the Internet inquirer. Once you do that, you then need to proceed and start investigating to find out what it is exactly that you can help the consumer with in order to get him or her one step closer to a vehicle purchase and into your dealership. Once you have given all the requested information, your goal is to book an appointment with the guest so that he or she can test drive the vehicle. Another way to successfully reply to the Internet inquiry if the guest who is inquiring happens to be out of town is to get the guest on the phone to fill out a credit application so that you can submit a preapproval. Use the same pitch as you would if you were taking a sales call. In order to save the guest time and an extra trip, get the deal approved prior to the guest coming into the dealership.

If a guest is inquiring about a new vehicle, that person will usually ask about specific options and availability. Same concept applies—answer all the person's questions and book an appointment to get him or her through the door.

*Price Inquiries*

When you get an inquiry about the price of a vehicle, the most ineffective way to handle this type of inquiry is to avoid giving the consumer a price. That is the old-school way of thinking. If someone wants a price, you give them the price. Why would you try and hide the price? A consumer needs to know the information. If the consumer feels like you are trying to hide the price, that person will lose faith in you and your dealership. If you get an inquiry on a new car, it's never a bad idea to reply with a price on every different trim level that the particular model comes in. This will give your customer a good idea of what kind of options and trim levels he or she thinks are affordable. The same goes for used cars, but for the most part, used car dealers have their used vehicles priced online. And if they don't, they should! When you get a price inquiry on a used car, make sure to reply with a price. The key is to be able to reply with the answer and then send back a hook question. A hook question looks something like this:

jamescrosby@hmail.com

"Hello, I was just wondering what the price is on the 2010 Acura TSX you guys have listed on your website. You guys have a stock number listed but no price???"

dereksaqqa@go.ca

"Hey, James! Thanks for the e-mail! I just got onto my website and found the vehicle you are inquiring about. That Acura TSX you inquired about is listed for $18,687.00. It's new to our inventory and is still available. The price hasn't been loaded online yet. I actually have a couple more comparable vehicles in stock as well. Were you specifically looking for a 2010 Acura TSX, or are you looking for something comparable in a certain price range?"

That's a quick example of a hook question. Whenever an Internet guest asks you a question, you need to respond with an answer to his or her question, then ask a follow-up question to keep the guest engaged in conversation. Here's one more example of a hook question:

Jamescrosby@hmail.com

"Hello, I have a couple questions about your 2011 Ford F150 you have advertised for $24,987.00. My first question is why are you guys asking $24,987.00 when I found three vehicles with the same options and kilometers for a lower price at other stores? My second question is, if I were to do business with you guys, is your price negotiable?"

dereksaqqa@go.ca

"Hey, James! Thanks for inquiring about our 2011 Ford F150. I appreciate you taking the time to ask about our pricing system. Our dealership strives to price all of our vehicles competitively within the local market. Having such a large market to compete with, it's very hard for us to always be the lowest price. We consistently do our research to make sure that we are priced fairly among all of our competitors. I can tell you in full confidence that we are not over-priced, but if you feel like you should be getting a better deal, I understand. In regards to having a negotiable price, that is something we would consider when you come down to the dealership and test drive the vehicle. Since the vehicle is preowned, I think it would be great if you could come down and check it out for yourself. The condition of the vehicle will play a big part in whether or not it's going to be the right one for you. Were you planning on coming by today to view the vehicle, or does tomorrow work better for you?"

Use those examples as a reference the next time you have a consumer who sends a price inquiry. Remember to always give the consumer a price and have a great pitch to justify why the price is what it is. Just like all other leads, your ultimate goal is to book an appointment with the guest and get him or her into your dealership. You need to be genuine and upfront and as helpful as possible to earn enough trust to get the Internet buyer from his or her home and into your store. The more trust you can establish, the more likely the buyer is to commit to his or her appointment.

*Offers*

A lot of consumers are more comfortable negotiating online where they are in their own comfort zone, whether that's at home or from their workplace. Often when these consumers inquire, they will throw an offer at you and see if you will go for it. There are two types of offers. There are lowball offers and genuine offers. If you are dealing with someone who is trying to lowball (extremely low offer) you on one of your vehicles, simply ask that person to justify his or her offer. If the person can justify his or her offer by proving that your vehicle is priced way too high in comparison to what else is out there in the market, then it would make sense to reconsider the offer and move forward and book an appointment. On the other hand, if the person can't justify his or her offer, then simply refuse the offer and explain that your vehicle is priced accordingly within the market. You should still look to book the customer in for an appointment so that you can try to close a deal, but just make sure that he or she isn't coming down expecting to get the vehicle for a ridiculous price. If you don't get the person through the door, then it was never going to amount to a deal anyway, so don't be too hard on yourself.

Now let's deal with the genuine offer. A genuine offer is an offer that isn't out of the realm of possibility. It's an offer lower than your asking price to get the negotiations rolling. One thing about the car industry is that consumers are prone to negotiate. It's almost as if people negotiate for bragging rights on who was a stronger negotiator and who got a better deal on their last vehicle purchase. If it's a realistic offer, you never want to refuse or accept the offer right away. It's a very difficult task to negotiate over the Internet. Your first objective is to compliment the offer and explain that the offer will be considered after the customer comes down to the dealership and physically demonstrates the vehicle. Let the customer know that if he or she drives the vehicle and decides that it's the one for him or her, then you will revisit the offer and come to terms on a deal. If the offer comes in on a new car and the guest has already driven the same model at a different dealership and is just looking for you to beat that dealership's deal, then take the opportunity to close the deal right then. Let the customer know that you are prepared to accept the offer conditioned on a deposit over the phone, and book him or her to come down to the store as soon as possible to start the paperwork. If the customer can't commit to giving you the deposit over the phone, then he or she isn't done price shopping.

*Trade-in Leads*

A trade-in lead is another common type of lead. Typically, when you get a trade-in lead, a consumer is inquiring about his or her trade-in value or even just trying to find out if your dealership would consider taking his or her vehicle in on trade or not. This is just another opening for you to start your sales process. The same principles apply with these kinds of leads just like with any other. When a consumer sends in a trade-in inquiry, that person inputs all of his or her current vehicle's information (year, make, model, kilometers, etc.) into the inquiry and requests a trade evaluation based off of the information submitted. In most cases, the consumer will have selected a desired vehicle that he or she is interested in buying.

It's very important to answer the inquiry with an evaluation on the trade-in value, but remember that people who are submitting trade-in leads are usually price shopping their current vehicle and trying to find out which dealer is willing to offer the most money. Don't shoot yourself in the foot and answer with an accurate number! I'm not saying to give the person an inaccurate number either. It wouldn't make sense for you and the dealer to be able to put an accurate number on a trade-in without having an opportunity to do a proper vehicle appraisal at the dealership. So when you are responding with a trade-in value, you always need to give a number that ranges from low to high. If you know, based off of the information you have received on the trade-in, that the vehicle is worth roughly $8,000, give an in and around number of $6,000 all the way to $12,000, subject to your dealer's vehicle appraisal. What this will do is create urgency from the consumer to come down to the dealership to get his or her vehicle appraised with the hopes of getting up to $12,000 for the trade. If you tell the consumer right from the get-go that his or her vehicle is worth roughly $8,000, then the consumer may not be happy with that number and may opt to keep submitting trade-in inquiries to other dealers until he or she hears a number that he or she feels is substantial enough to get him or her to book a solid appointment with you to get the vehicle appraised. Make sure to never commit to a trade-in value prior to ever seeing the vehicle; it could come back to bite you.

Once you give the consumer peace of mind on his or her trade-in value, you can then continue to get into the consumer's vehicle of interest and start to get that person excited about his or her new vehicle purchase.

*Credit Inquiries*

A credit lead is one of the most common inquires for consumers who have poor credit history. In a lot of dealerships, there is separation between the Internet department and the credit department. The credit department is basically focused on subprime consumers. If you are a member of the credit department, you are going to be working the deal from front to back, meaning that you will get the lead, submit the application to the bank, and then bring your guest down to select a vehicle once you have received an approval. With credit inquiries, it will sometimes take longer to get an approval and have all the stipulations satisfied by the lender. Subprime consumers are required to provide lots more information than prime consumers. In most cases, subprime consumers will need to provide paystubs and job letters. Sometimes they need previous employment records, bank statements, along with T4s and notices of assessment. What is needed all depends on the consumer's current working situation. If the individual had previous bankruptcies, he or she will need to provide discharge letters and trustee letters. This is all information the lenders will request depending on the extent of the applicant's credit history. This is why it takes longer to get a confirmed approval for subprime consumers because of all the documentation that must be provided by these individuals.

People who submit credit leads are basically asking you to get them approved so that they can purchase a vehicle. They know that they have poor credit history, so they just want to know the best rates they can be offered and how much money the lending institutions are willing to lend them. In order for you to be productive and have a high closing ratio on these leads, you need to understand the process and be able to explain the steps to each individual guest. Be prepared for a lot of paperwork because you will be submitting a lot of applications. The key is to be able to get each and every credit inquirer to believe that you are going to get him or her approved on his or her desired vehicle, or a vehicle as close to what is desired. From the initial point of contact, you need to get these people to trust you and not shop around. The only way to do this is to win them over with your confidence. The more confident you are about getting them approved, the more confident they will be with you and your dealership and the less likely they will be to shop around. If you get a credit lead and you open the consumer's credit bureau and know that you are going to require a little bit extra documentation from the applicant, be straight with the consumer and tell him or her, "Hey, I'm going to get you into a vehicle. I'm sure of it! I just need you to help us out and get me these extra pieces of information because I know the lenders are going to ask for them. So if we work as a team, we can get this wrapped up in the next couple of days."

These are the consumers that you sometimes need to quarterback throughout the whole sale. Hold them accountable. If someone tells you that he or she is going to send you paystubs tomorrow at 9:00 a.m., make sure you express the importance of the paystubs and explain why you need them. Come 9:00 a.m., if you don't have those paystubs, give the guest a call and let him or her know that you and the banks are expecting them. This is where your follow-up skills will come into play because these are the types of clients that you need to touch base with on a daily basis to give them updates and check up on how gathering the required documentation is coming along. The more applications you are working at a time, the more organized you have to be. Don't forget to follow up with these applicants because they will be quick to jump ship the second they feel like you are not taking them seriously.

# Internet Tips

1. When a guest asks you several questions about any particular vehicle or financing options, make sure to answer each and every question. If you neglect to answer any of the several questions asked, you may give off the impression that you are intentionally not answering one of the guest's questions for a reason.

2. Always have a captivating subject line when you are sending out a new e-mail. The more unique and interesting a subject line you can create, the better your chances of catching the attention of your recipient. If you are dealing with a guest who receives a handful of e-mails per day, you want yours to jump out at him or her every time. So the more unique you make the subject line, the more intrigued the recipient will be to open your e-mail.

3. Always look to get the consumer to make the transition from the Internet, where they are thinking logically (meaning that they are just looking at prices and pictures), to the phone or into the dealership so that you can get them emotionally involved with the purchase. Consumers make purchases based off their emotions. It's hard to get a guest emotionally attached to a vehicle or to you without getting that person into the dealership to meet you and take a vehicle out for a test drive. The test drive is when any guest reaches his or her emotional high throughout every car deal. After the test drive, when your guest is excited, he or she will start to make decisions based off his or her emotions. That's why a test drive is one of the most important steps in the selling process.

4. Book an appointment! Any time you have an Internet inquiry, never forget what your ultimate goal is. Appointment, appointment, appointment. Get the consumer through the door and start your sales process.

5. Master the hook questions. A hook question is basically a follow-up question to any questions an Internet inquirer asks you. First, you respond with an answer and follow up with a question of your own. Ask the same questions you would ask as if you were taking a sales call or filling out a guest sheet with a walk-in guest. In all scenarios, you are driving toward the same finish line and navigating your way to a car deal.

6. The faster you respond to an Internet lead, the better chance you have at closing a deal. Make sure you respond to every lead within the first five minutes of receiving it. The longer you wait to respond to a lead, the colder it gets. Always be ready and able to respond to an Internet lead at any given time and place. Put yourself on a timer every time a lead comes in. You are on the clock, and every second counts!

7. Having templates ready to send out to all your Internet inquirers is a great idea. Just make sure to personalize every e-mail you send out by adding names and any other personal information you may have collected throughout your back-and-forth e-mails.

8. When you're dealing with credit applicants, you're going to run into situations where you will have guests inquiring about vehicles that are priced upward of $20,000. Never let a guest know right off the bat that you will not be able to get him or her into the vehicle that he or she inquired about. If the person applies for a vehicle that you know will be out of his or her price range, let that person know that you will send it off to the lenders and try to get him or her approved on it. This way the consumer will continue to wait for you to get him or her approved, and they will be more inclined to collect all the paperwork for you that you are requesting from them. If you tell these consumers that they have no chance of getting into the vehicle they want, they will be less committed to you and more likely to stop answering your calls and start applying with one of your competitors.

9. Don't try and negotiate a car deal and payments via e-mail. You will never win, and your dealership will never make money. The art of closing payments is best served face-to-face. Closing a deal while the guest is at the dealership will always prove more effective over trying to get it done over e-mail. The art of closing face-to-face is something that will never die in the car industry.

10. Master the computer basics. You can't be effective on the computer without being able to utilize everything it's got to offer. Think outside the box and go the extra mile when you're dealing with Internet customers. Being able to do simple things like attach links to websites or attach vehicle pictures, sending quick one- or two-minute videos of a vehicle walk-around, or being able to send out customized templates to any given Internet prospect at any given time will give you the edge against you're competitors. This should go without saying, but there are still salespeople out there who claim to be great in the Internet department, yet they aren't able to capitalize on these quick-and-easy tools that are right at their fingertips, literally. These are the little things that will make the biggest impact on your customer service and overall sales.

11. Always do some research on your competition in your downtime. When you have a guest comparing your vehicle with that of your competitors, it's always good to know about your competitor's product so that you can help sway your guest to make the right decision based on facts that you can provide. Just like your manufacturer's rebates and incentives are changing, so are all the other manufacturers' offers.

# Chapter 6:
# Motives and Goal Setting

*"My number one goal is to turn my dreams into my realities."*

*"Impossible is nothing." – Muhammad Ali*

At last we've arrived at the final chapter. I want you to ask yourself, *What is my biggest motivational tool? What drives me to get up every morning and do the best I can in any situation I face? How much hard work am I willing to put in? How far do I see myself taking my career?* These are all very important questions that you need to take some time and think about before you answer them. Don't answer them just yet! At the end of this chapter, go back to these questions and put in a solid answer for each one of them.

A long time ago, somebody told me that unless I knew what I was working toward, I wouldn't be able to gauge whether or not I was successful in achieving what I was working toward. It took me a couple years to understand what that really meant. I realized that in order to keep myself grounded and on track, I needed to set goals for myself instead of just waking up every day and going to work with the mentality "I'm going to sell a car today" or "I'm going to make lots of money without any real plans or goals for the day, month, or year." So I started to plan my days. That way when I started my days, I would know exactly what I was going to do on any given day. I gave myself goals for each day. Whether it was to take four ups and close two deals, or make twenty follow-up calls and call twenty of my previous guests, or give myself a thirty-minute break to do some training, I always had a plan that needed to be executed, and my day would not have been successful unless I had completed everything I had set out to achieve that day.

How can you track your success if you have no goals or targets to aim for? It all starts with planning out your day, then planning out what you want to achieve for the month, then setting what you want your yearly target to be, and so on. You need to implement short-term and long-term goals in your life. You need to have a target to aim for. You need to be working toward a certain accomplishment that you set in place for yourself.

This is nothing new to anyone. I'm not the first person to talk about goal setting and creating personal targets. I am just reiterating the fact that unless you do these things, you will not learn and grow to your fullest potential. In my past experience, I've learned that not only do you grow to become stronger and more organized when you set goals for yourself, but once you understand how effective goal setting is, you will start to use your goals, along with your daily, monthly, and yearly plans, as your guideline or map, if you will. It will become easier for you to stay on track and not let anything distract you or slow you down from your conquest.

> *Tip: Don't set a goal just to say that you set a goal. You need to really want to obtain a goal. To effectively set goals and work toward achieving them, you need to take time to set the goal, write it down in your journal or daytime planner, and then draw out how you are going to go about reaching that goal. When you write down long-term goals, make sure you review these goals every other month just as a reminder for yourself. This way you won't forget these bigger goals, and at the same time you can check to see whether you are on track in achieving them.*

Let's start setting some daily goals and at the same time gain understanding about why it's important to do so. Let's keep the focus on work-related goals even though this is a great way to execute your daily responsibilities outside of work too. If you're going to work every day and the only thing you have planned for the day is taking ups, then there's a problem. Any successful salesperson will tell you that he or she has his or her day planned out from the second he or she walks into the dealership.

Successful salespeople know what vehicles they need to get ready for deliveries, they know what vehicles they need to talk to their service department about, they know exactly which guests they need to call, and they know exactly how many appointments they have for the day. Good salespeople will have vehicles ready for viewing in anticipation of their appointments and will already be thinking of plan B vehicles just in case their guests aren't sold on the first option. These are basic day-to-day activities that you need to be on top of to ensure a successful day.

Most dealerships have computer systems such as CRM or Higher Gear, and there are a couple more systems like these that are used by dealers that will help you organize information about your workday. These are all great systems that are tried, tested, and true.

Let's go above and beyond. Even though you are more than likely utilizing one of those computer systems, it's never a bad idea to keep a daily planner by your side at all times. A daily planner will allow you to write down all your responsibilities for the day, and you can also prioritize which responsibilities are most important for you to get done. Your daily planner will also act as a reminder for you if you need to make an important call or if you are away from the dealership and talk to a guest. You can jot down some important notes from your conversation, and that way when you get back to the dealership, you will remember what you needed to do in regards to the conversation with your guest. Also, when you write down all the responsibilities you have to accomplish on any given day and check them off as you complete them, you get yourself in the habit of completing your tasks. These day-to-day goals or tasks are just the beginning of a highly effective strategy used to get yourself trained and ready to start setting bigger and broader goals for yourself and executing them. Ultimately, by prioritizing your day-to-day activities and getting them out of the way, you free up more time for you to focus on your other goals, such as generating more business.

Get yourself a daily planner and start using it today. Watch how quickly you go from being disorganized to having complete structure to all of your days. Daily planning is going to keep you one step ahead of the game at all times. Once you get into the habit of daily planning, you will be ready to take the next step.

Once you are in the habit of structuring your days in a way in which you are utilizing your time effectively and completing all your daily priorities and goals, you now need to focus on your monthly targets and how you should be structuring your month. It's all about accountability! It's one thing to say that your goal is to sell twenty cars next month, but it's another thing to say that you are going to sell twenty cars next month *and* you have a monthly sales plan to get you there. This would be a bigger goal that you can continually track month to month to see how successful you are. Don't wait for your manager to set these goals for you. Set these goals on your own, and take ownership of them. By setting your own goals and targets for the month, it will be easier for you to focus on what you're doing, and then you can determine how much work and time you need to put in so that you can reach your monthly target. I'm going to give you a monthly sales plan reference guide to follow. I'm going to go over all the different areas you can use to generate car deals. This way, when you draw up your monthly sales plan, you can be held accountable for your progress. Let's start by going over the eight different areas from which you can look to generate car deals.

### 1. Walk-in customers (ups)

Walk-in traffic is one of the most popular sources of business. For you salespeople working on the sales floor, walk-in traffic is one of the biggest areas you will rely on to generate business. This is where you will start to build your clientele base and your reputation.

## 2. Sales calls (phone leads)

Sales calls are another primary source of business. By now, you should have already mastered the art of taking sales calls from my sales call scripts given in Chapter 3. Sales calls are basically phone leads. They are just another form of customer inquiry. These are the guests who choose to inquire about a vehicle via telephone as opposed to the Internet.

## 3. Internet leads

I put Internet leads and credit leads under the same category. Internet business has taken a huge leap and is growing stronger and stronger all the time. Get yourself on the Internet bus because these leads can be very fruitful, if you learn how to handle them properly. A lot of salespeople only use this form of networking to generate business, and it has proven to be very successful.

## 4. Repeat business

Repeat business is a great source of business with the highest closing ratio. The reason why there is such a high success rate with repeat business is that guest relationships have already been established. The guest is coming back to buy another vehicle from you, so he or she already trusts you. Repeat business is not that easy to come by. You need to establish a clientele base through great customer service, and you need to have some time under your belt too. The more seasoned you are, the broader your clientele base will be, and, in return, your repeat business will start to increase. Make sure to start your dealer tracker if you have not already done so in order to stay organized and on top of your repeat opportunities. (Refer to Chapter 4 under Repeat and Referral Business to get your deal tracker started.)

## 5. Referral business

Start your referral program! Referral business is also one of the sources that will return one of the highest closing ratios. Just like repeat business, the trust level between you and your referred guest has already been established by the person who referred you. Once you have that trust level built, it's easier for you to close the deal. Referral business is not easy to attain. It needs to be earned through great customer service. If you can start your referral programs and get yourself two referrals a month, that's a great start and a great accomplishment.

## 6. Service guests

This is an area of business that is known by all salespeople but often goes untapped by most of them. Generating business from your service guests is not as hard as you might think. The reason why a lot of salespeople aren't doing it is because it doesn't have the best success rate. It's got one of the lowest closing ratios, which means as a salesperson, you will get a lot of rejection in this sector. Think about it this way. If you have nothing better to do than hang out in the service department talking to your previous guests about potentially upgrading their vehicles, then why not do it? Start by committing to closing one service guest per month. If you do that, you are on your way to earning commissions for twelve extra deals next year! I can't find anything wrong with that.

## 7. Self-networking

This is where you as a salesperson need to think outside the box and start networking yourself some business. Your dealership will provide you with all the other sources of business. Start thinking of ways to market yourself and get your name out there. It's a small world, and word of mouth travels quickly. Don't be afraid to hand out business cards to random people and promote the fact that you are in the car industry and you are waiting to serve your next guest. There are plenty of ways to network yourself and promote your business. Do some research to find ways that you can network yourself and have fun all at the same time. Self-promoting, when done properly, can open doors to new business that you never thought possible. Try it out and see what happens.

## 8. Be-backs

A be-back guest is someone who has been at your dealership once or twice but still hasn't closed deal with you. These guests are guests who you find yourself following up with for a little bit longer than usual for several reasons. It could be that they are out of town and too busy to come down to the dealership, or they are just not quick to commit and are waiting for you to find them the perfect vehicle. There are many reasons for you to have guests that fall into the be-back category. Strong follow-up is what will get them back through the door. Make sure you go through all your prospects daily and try to find another angle to take with them so that you can get them back into the dealership to make a deal. There is a good closing ratio on these guests, so let the follow-up begin.

Now that I covered all the areas there are for you to utilize on your road to success in the car industry, I'm going to lay out a monthly sales chart that you should use to track your monthly targets and that will provide a guideline for you to see how and from where you are going to get your deals. This chart is going to help you gauge what areas you are strongest in and what areas you are going to have to develop so that you can get to the next level of salesmanship. Look at the example chart below, and then I will explain what each column is designed to do.

# Monthly Sales Chart

|  | # of deals | CR | total leads | X2/50% tubed | month end total | # of deals | ACR |
|---|---|---|---|---|---|---|---|
| Walk-Ins, Ups |  | 20% |  |  |  |  |  |
| Sales Calls |  | 50% |  |  |  |  |  |
| Internet Leads |  | 50% |  |  |  |  |  |
| Repeat Business |  | 75% |  |  |  |  |  |
| Referral Business |  | 50% |  |  |  |  |  |
| Service Guests |  | 50% |  |  |  |  |  |
| Self-networking |  | 50% |  |  |  |  |  |
| Be-Backs |  | 50% |  |  |  |  |  |
| **Target** |  |  |  |  |  |  |  |

**# Of deals**. In this column, you need to put the number of deals you are targeting to get from each source of business.

**Closing ratio**. This number is the average closing ratio for each source of business.

**Total leads**. Based off of the number of deals you are targeting to attain multiplied by the closing ratio for each source of business, this should be the total amount of leads or guests you need to contact in order to achieve your target.

**Tube ratio**. This number is your current tube ratio. In my example, I am using a 50 percent ratio, which is higher than the average tube ratio. So if your tube ratio is 50 percent, then you need to add 50 percent to the number of leads you calculated based off of your number of deals to closing ratio.

**Month end total**. This is the total amount of leads that you have contacted at the end of the month. (This number is generated from another chart that I will show you right away. The next chart will show you how to track how many people you have contacted for every source of business.)

**# of deals closed**. In this column, you need to fill out your actual number of sold deals per source at the end of the month.

**Actual closing ratio**. This number is calculated by the number of actual deals sold based of the number of leads contacted throughout the month. This will get you your personal closing ratio for every source of business.

Now take a look at my daily tracker. This tracking system will allow you to manually put in the number of leads received per source. This chart needs to be by your side at all times. Always have it on hand so that you can properly track your leads. This whole system is dependent on whether or not you are accurate and truthful throughout the month while filling out your monthly tracker daily.

# Daily Tracker

| | | | | | | | | | | |
|---|---|---|---|---|---|---|---|---|---|---|
| W | W | W | W | W | W | W | W | W | W | |
| SC | SC | SC | SC | SC | SC | SC | SC | SC | SC | |
| IL | IL | IL | IL | IL | IL | IL | IL | IL | IL | |
| RP B | RP B | RP B | RP B | RP B | RP B | RP B | RP B | RP B | RP B | |
| RF B | B | RF B | B | B | B | RF B | RF B | RF B | RF B | |
| E | E | E | E | E | E | E | E | E | E | |
| SN | SN | SN | SN | SN | SN | SN | SN | SN | SN | |
| BB | BB | BB | BB | BB | BB | BB | BB | BB | BB | |
| DS | DS | DS | DS | DS | DS | DS | DS | DS | DS | |

W: WALK-IN/UPS SC: SALES CALLS IL: INTERNET LEADS
RPB: REPEAT BUSINESS RFB: REFERFAL BUSINESS
E: EXCHANGE SN: SELF NETWORKING BB: BE-BACKS
DS: DEALS SUBMITTED

Take a look at the legend under the chart. Make sure you fill out your daily tracker accurately at the end of every workday. Refer back to this chart at the end of the month, and fill out your monthly sales chart. This is going to allow you to visually see what sectors you excelled in and what sectors you failed to reach your target. This will to help you identify your weak areas and will allow you to know what areas you need to focus on next month. The ultimate goal is for you to grow in all areas and get yourself into a position where you are hitting all your targets in all the different sectors.

Now that we've covered daily goal setting and monthly goal setting, let's get into yearly goal setting. Yearly goals should be goals that you have set

for yourself that you feel are attainable. Don't set your targets too low, yet
don't set them too high either. Review your previous track record, along
with your newly acquired monthly planner, and actually take some time
to come up with realistic target for the year. Your daily organization
habits plus your monthly sales charts should help you evaluate and stay
on track to reaching your annual target.

Above and beyond your sales volume target, add some personal goals,
along with other business goals, in your yearly plan. You may have a
goal to become more educated in the car industry, or your goal may
be to save$ 50,000 to put down on your first home. Whatever the goal
is, you need to plan out what steps you are going to take to get your
plan into action. Follow the same principles you would as if you were
tracking your sales volume. The same process can be applied to personal health goals and so on. When you are setting goals, make sure
not to overwhelm yourself with too many. If you do, it's going to be
very easy to lose direction. Focus on one or two major goals that you
would like to accomplish, and work toward completing them. At that
point, you can look to set another set of important goals and tackle
them two at time. When you are setting your goals, you need to really
want them. Once you decide what's most important to you, you need
to map out the road to the finish line. Don't let your day-to-day operations consume all your time and allow you to lose focus on your major
goals. Once you start implementing goal setting in your life, you will
be on the right path to success. Keep a strong mind and always be
working toward something. That way you will never get lost on your
journey.

## The Dos and Don'ts of Car Sales

Here's a quick list of things salespeople should always be doing and a list
of things salespeople should never be doing. Enjoy!

Do:

- Be grateful for all the business you receive.

- Listen to understand customer motives, needs, and wants.

- Say hi to every guest you run into.

- Stay positive.

- Follow the sales process.

- Enjoy following up with guests.

- Be punctual.

- Ask questions.

- Control the sale.

- Always be smiling.

- Make your guests feel comfortable.

- Invest in educating yourself.

- Training, training, training.

- Master your people skills.

- Have lots of product knowledge.

- Take every opportunity you find.

- Dress to impress. Look good + Feel good = Sell good.

- Sell with enthusiasm.

- Help out your team members.

- Use a guest sheet.

- Utilize your manager.

- Properly represent your company.

- Be on top of your deliveries.

- Qualify your guests.

- Be professional.

- Be a problem solver.

- Close the deal.

Don't:

- Take anything personally.

- Be pushy.

- Lose control of the sale.

- Neglect your guests.

- Forget to follow up.

- Interrupt your guests.

- Speak over your guest.

- Be negative.

- Worry about what other people are doing.

- Be unprofessional.

- Never prequalify a guest before talking to him or her.

- Be unreasonable with team members.

- Ever have nothing to do.

- Make promises you can't keep.

- Make promises you don't intend to keep.

- Miss an opportunity to deliver a vehicle to your guest.

- Speak in an unprofessional manner.

- Present numbers without getting commitment to the vehicle.

- Miss an opportunity to go with your guests on a test drive.

- Think only of yourself.

- Fear rejection.

- Fear the word *no*.

- Lose confidence.

- Talk badly about your competition.

- Discuss finance terms until the guest is approved and at the dealership.

- Let a guest leave without manager turnover.

- Be a circle jerker.

- Be unproductive.

- Overpromise or underdeliver.

- Lose your passion for selling.

- Get discouraged.

- Forget about all the great things we have in life because of all the guests who told you yes!

# Conclusion: Keep the Fire Burning

*"If my mind can conceive it, and my heart*
*can believe it, then I can achieve it."*
*– Muhammad Ali*

Everybody has a purpose in life. In this life, you are measured by a lot of things. Among them are your successes. There has got to be a burning desire to want to be the best and excel at anything and everything you do if you are going to survive your climb to the top of the food chain in the car business. You need to be a warrior, relentless on your pursuit to the top. If you want to master the game, you need to kick it into high gear and get your grind on. There is no stopping, and there is no second place.

In order for you to keep the burning desire to succeed, you need to have a motivational tool—something that drives you to get up every morning and succeed. For some people, it's plain and simple: money is their motivation. For others, it's the desire to take care of their family and themselves. A lot of people are driven by self-worth—always reaching out to hit higher standards in life and setting out to accomplish what most people won't. One of the ultimate rewards is self-fulfillment— being able to leave a legacy behind, and before you leave, being able to say that you actually did something in your life that mattered. You need to have a purpose—a reason for being, seeing, and believing. Without any aspirations, you won't care to train, research, and develop your skills in business and in your personal life.

Now that you have all the tools you need to become successful in the world of cars, use them to your advantage and start earning a reputation of being a master salesperson. Always remember that you are going to have ups and downs, but at the end of the day, you are doing what you love to do, and that's all that matters. Use this industry to better yourself and the people around you.

The proof is in the pudding. You can have everything you ever dreamed of and more if you can *master the game.*

CPSIA information can be obtained at www.ICGtesting.com
Printed in the USA
BVOW03s1520250914

368357BV00012B/206/P